THE RIVALS
OF PAINFUL GULCH

BY MORRIS & GOSCINNY

Original title: Lucky Luke – Les rivaux de Painful Gulch
Original edition: © Dargaud Editeur Paris 1971 by Goscinny and Morris
© Lucky Comics
www.lucky-luke.com
English translation: © 2008 Cinebook Ltd
Translator: Luke Spear
Lettering and text layout: Imadjinn sarl
This edition first published in Great Britain in 2008 by
Cinebook Ltd
56 Beech Avenue
Canterbury, Kent
CT4 7TA
www.cinebook.com
Second printing: June 2016
Printed in Spain by EGEDSA
A CIP catalogue record for this book
is available from the British Library
ISBN 978-1-905460-60-1

9th CINEBOOK
The 9th Art Publisher

THE Rivals OF PAINFUL GULCH

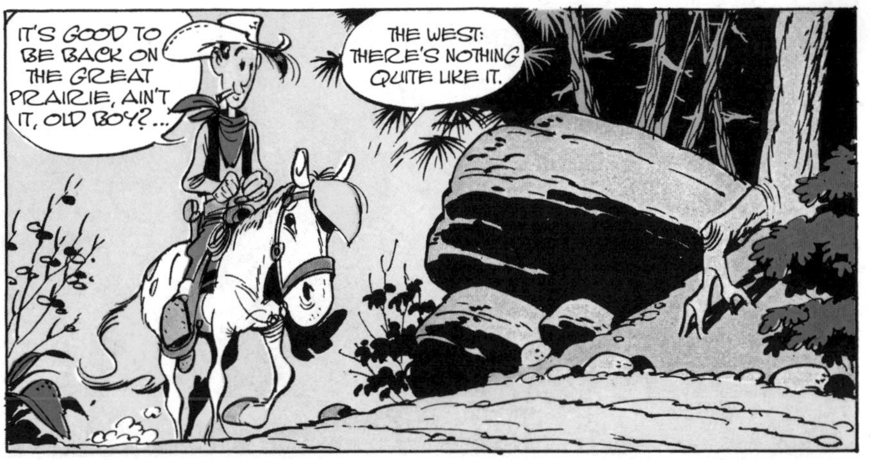

IT'S GOOD TO BE BACK ON THE GREAT PRAIRIE, AIN'T IT, OLD BOY?...
THE WEST: THERE'S NOTHING QUITE LIKE IT.

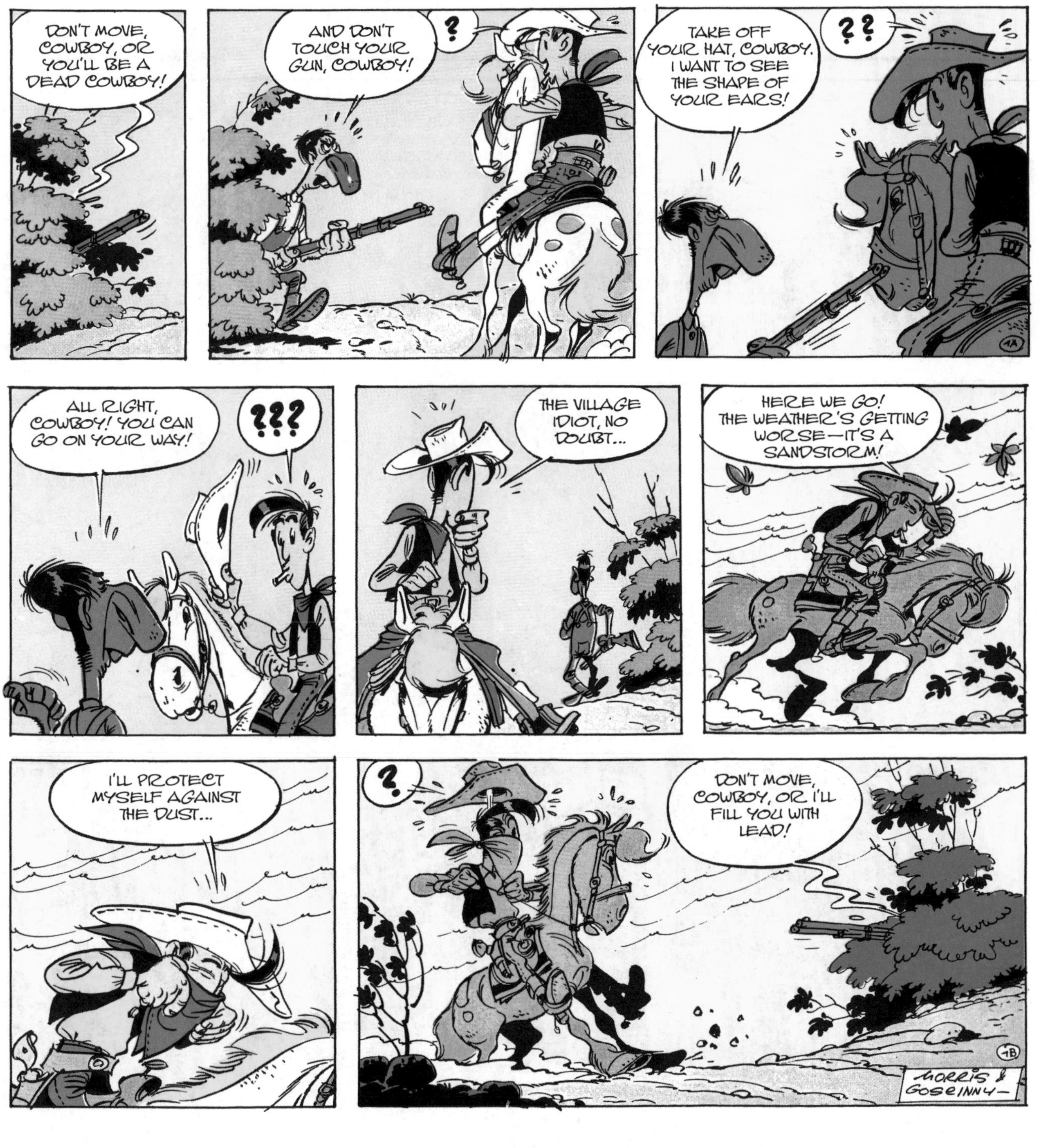

DON'T MOVE, COWBOY, OR YOU'LL BE A DEAD COWBOY!
AND DON'T TOUCH YOUR GUN, COWBOY!
?
TAKE OFF YOUR HAT, COWBOY. I WANT TO SEE THE SHAPE OF YOUR EARS!
??
ALL RIGHT, COWBOY! YOU CAN GO ON YOUR WAY!
???
THE VILLAGE IDIOT, NO DOUBT...
HERE WE GO! THE WEATHER'S GETTING WORSE—IT'S A SANDSTORM!
I'LL PROTECT MYSELF AGAINST THE DUST...
?
DON'T MOVE, COWBOY, OR I'LL FILL YOU WITH LEAD!
MORRIS & GOSCINNY

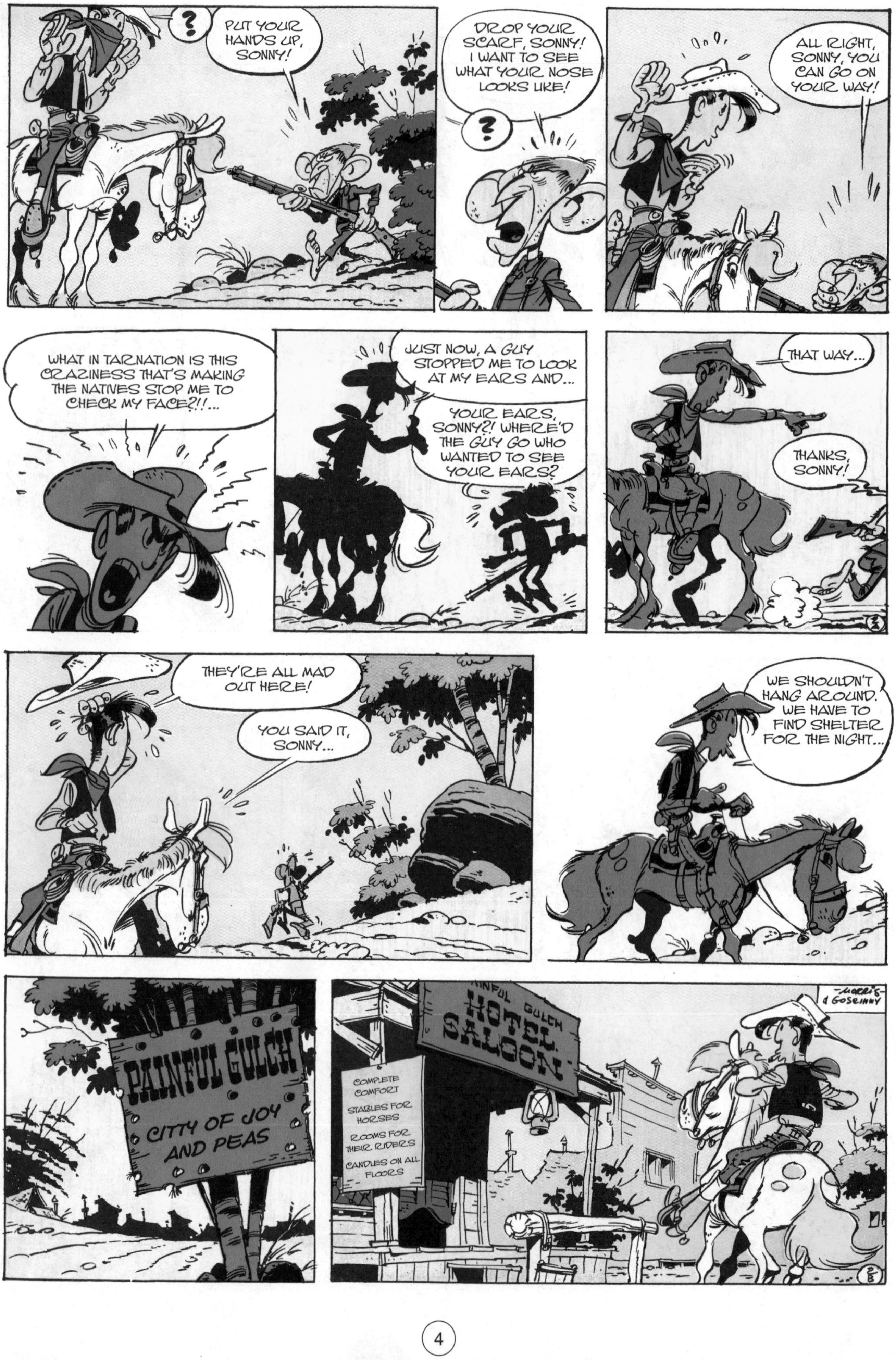
?
PUT YOUR HANDS UP, SONNY!
DROP YOUR SCARF, SONNY! I WANT TO SEE WHAT YOUR NOSE LOOKS LIKE!
?
ALL RIGHT, SONNY, YOU CAN GO ON YOUR WAY!
WHAT IN TARNATION IS THIS CRAZINESS THAT'S MAKING THE NATIVES STOP ME TO CHECK MY FACE?!!...
JUST NOW, A GUY STOPPED ME TO LOOK AT MY EARS AND...
YOUR EARS, SONNY?! WHERE'D THE GUY GO WHO WANTED TO SEE YOUR EARS?
THAT WAY...
THANKS, SONNY!
THEY'RE ALL MAD OUT HERE!
YOU SAID IT, SONNY...
WE SHOULDN'T HANG AROUND. WE HAVE TO FIND SHELTER FOR THE NIGHT...
PAINFUL GULCH
CITTY OF JOY AND PEAS
HOTEL SALOON
COMPLETE COMFORT
STABLES FOR HORSES
ROOMS FOR THEIR RIDERS
CANDLES ON ALL FLOORS
MORRIS & GOSCINNY

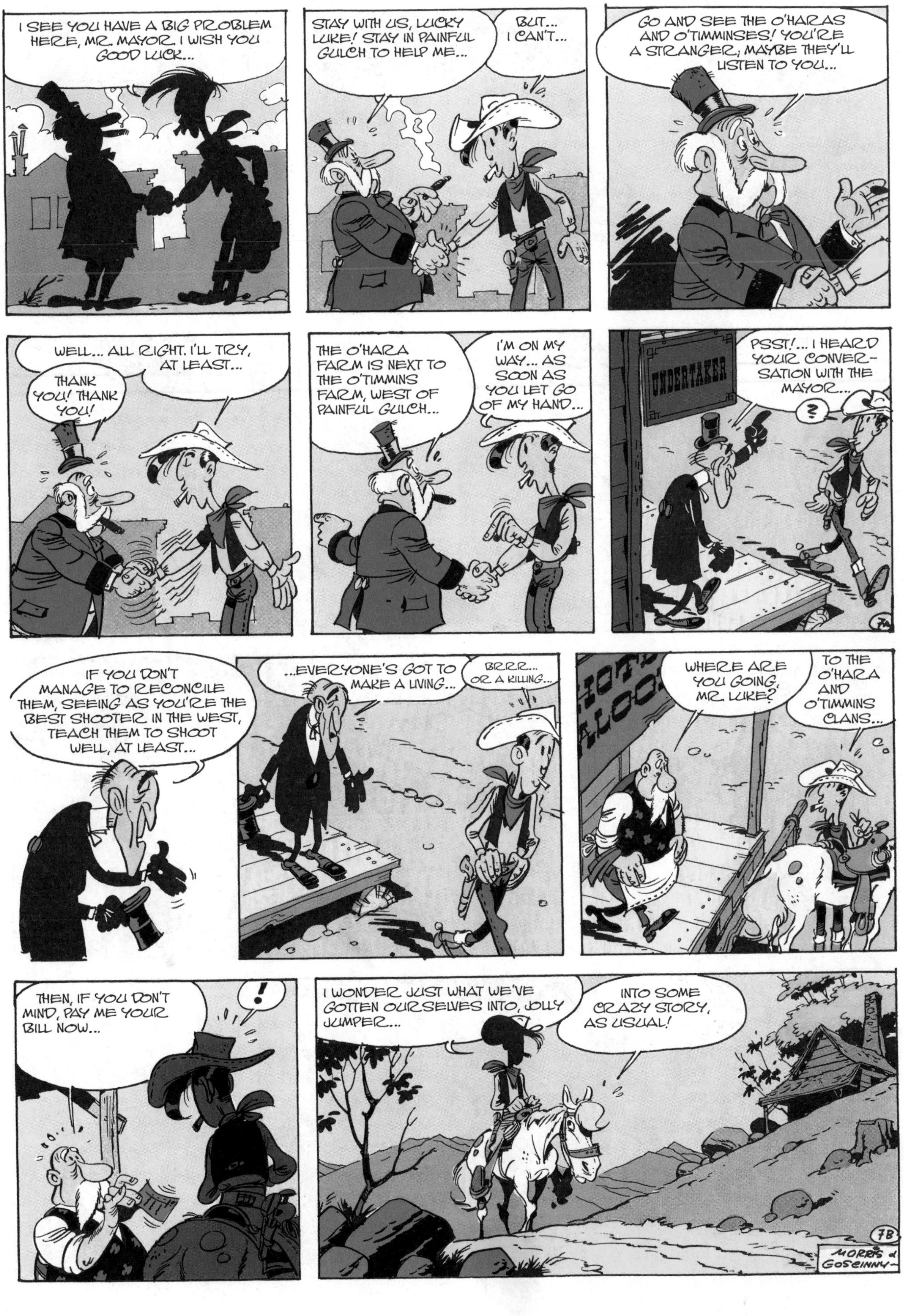
I SEE YOU HAVE A BIG PROBLEM HERE, MR. MAYOR. I WISH YOU GOOD LUCK...
STAY WITH US, LUCKY LUKE! STAY IN PAINFUL GULCH TO HELP ME...
BUT... I CAN'T...
GO AND SEE THE O'HARAS AND O'TIMMINSES! YOU'RE A STRANGER; MAYBE THEY'LL LISTEN TO YOU...
WELL... ALL RIGHT. I'LL TRY, AT LEAST...
THANK YOU! THANK YOU!
THE O'HARA FARM IS NEXT TO THE O'TIMMINS FARM, WEST OF PAINFUL GULCH...
I'M ON MY WAY... AS SOON AS YOU LET GO OF MY HAND...
UNDERTAKER
PSST!... I HEARD YOUR CONVERSATION WITH THE MAYOR...
?
7A
IF YOU DON'T MANAGE TO RECONCILE THEM, SEEING AS YOU'RE THE BEST SHOOTER IN THE WEST, TEACH THEM TO SHOOT WELL, AT LEAST...
...EVERYONE'S GOT TO MAKE A LIVING...
BRRR... OR A KILLING...
WHERE ARE YOU GOING, MR. LUKE?
TO THE O'HARA AND O'TIMMINS CLANS...
THEN, IF YOU DON'T MIND, PAY ME YOUR BILL NOW...
!
I WONDER JUST WHAT WE'VE GOTTEN OURSELVES INTO, JOLLY JUMPER...
INTO SOME CRAZY STORY, AS USUAL!
7B
MORRIS & GOSCINNY

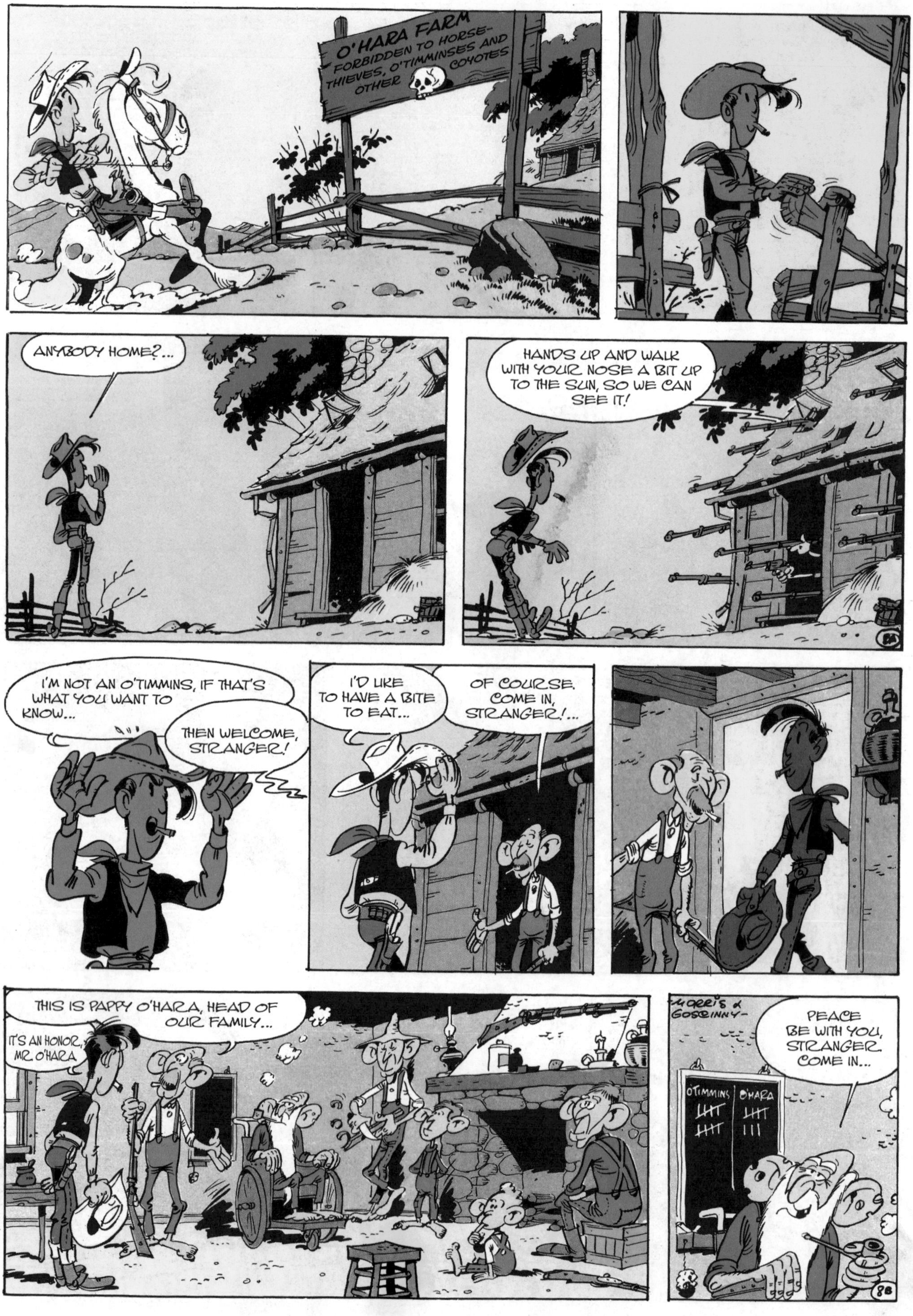
O'HARA FARM
FORBIDDEN TO HORSE-THIEVES, O'TIMMINSES AND OTHER COYOTES
ANYBODY HOME?...
HANDS UP AND WALK WITH YOUR NOSE A BIT UP TO THE SUN, SO WE CAN SEE IT!
I'M NOT AN O'TIMMINS, IF THAT'S WHAT YOU WANT TO KNOW...
THEN WELCOME, STRANGER!
I'D LIKE TO HAVE A BITE TO EAT...
OF COURSE. COME IN, STRANGER!...
THIS IS PAPPY O'HARA, HEAD OF OUR FAMILY...
IT'S AN HONOR, MR O'HARA
MORRIS & GOSCINNY
O'TIMMINS
O'HARA
PEACE BE WITH YOU, STRANGER COME IN...

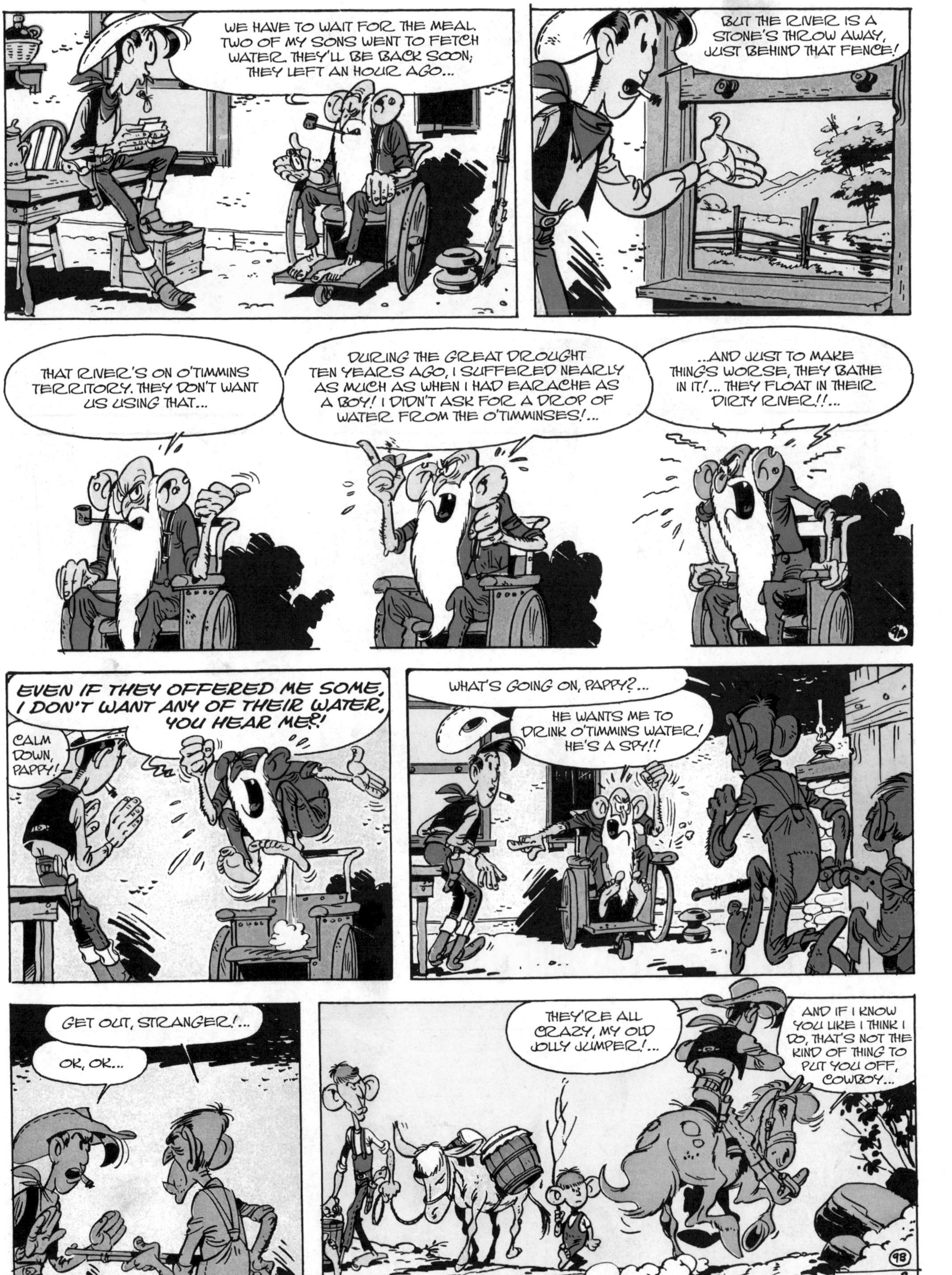
WE HAVE TO WAIT FOR THE MEAL. TWO OF MY SONS WENT TO FETCH WATER. THEY'LL BE BACK SOON; THEY LEFT AN HOUR AGO...
BUT THE RIVER IS A STONE'S THROW AWAY, JUST BEHIND THAT FENCE!
THAT RIVER'S ON O'TIMMINS TERRITORY. THEY DON'T WANT US USING THAT...
DURING THE GREAT DROUGHT TEN YEARS AGO, I SUFFERED NEARLY AS MUCH AS WHEN I HAD EARACHE AS A BOY! I DIDN'T ASK FOR A DROP OF WATER FROM THE O'TIMMINSES!...
...AND JUST TO MAKE THINGS WORSE, THEY BATHE IN IT!... THEY FLOAT IN THEIR DIRTY RIVER!!...
EVEN IF THEY OFFERED ME SOME, I DON'T WANT ANY OF THEIR WATER, YOU HEAR ME?!
CALM DOWN, PAPPY!
WHAT'S GOING ON, PAPPY?...
HE WANTS ME TO DRINK O'TIMMINS WATER! HE'S A SPY!!
GET OUT, STRANGER!...
OK, OK...
THEY'RE ALL CRAZY, MY OLD JOLLY JUMPER!...
AND IF I KNOW YOU LIKE I THINK I DO, THAT'S NOT THE KIND OF THING TO PUT YOU OFF, COWBOY...
98
-MORRIS-
GOSCINNY-

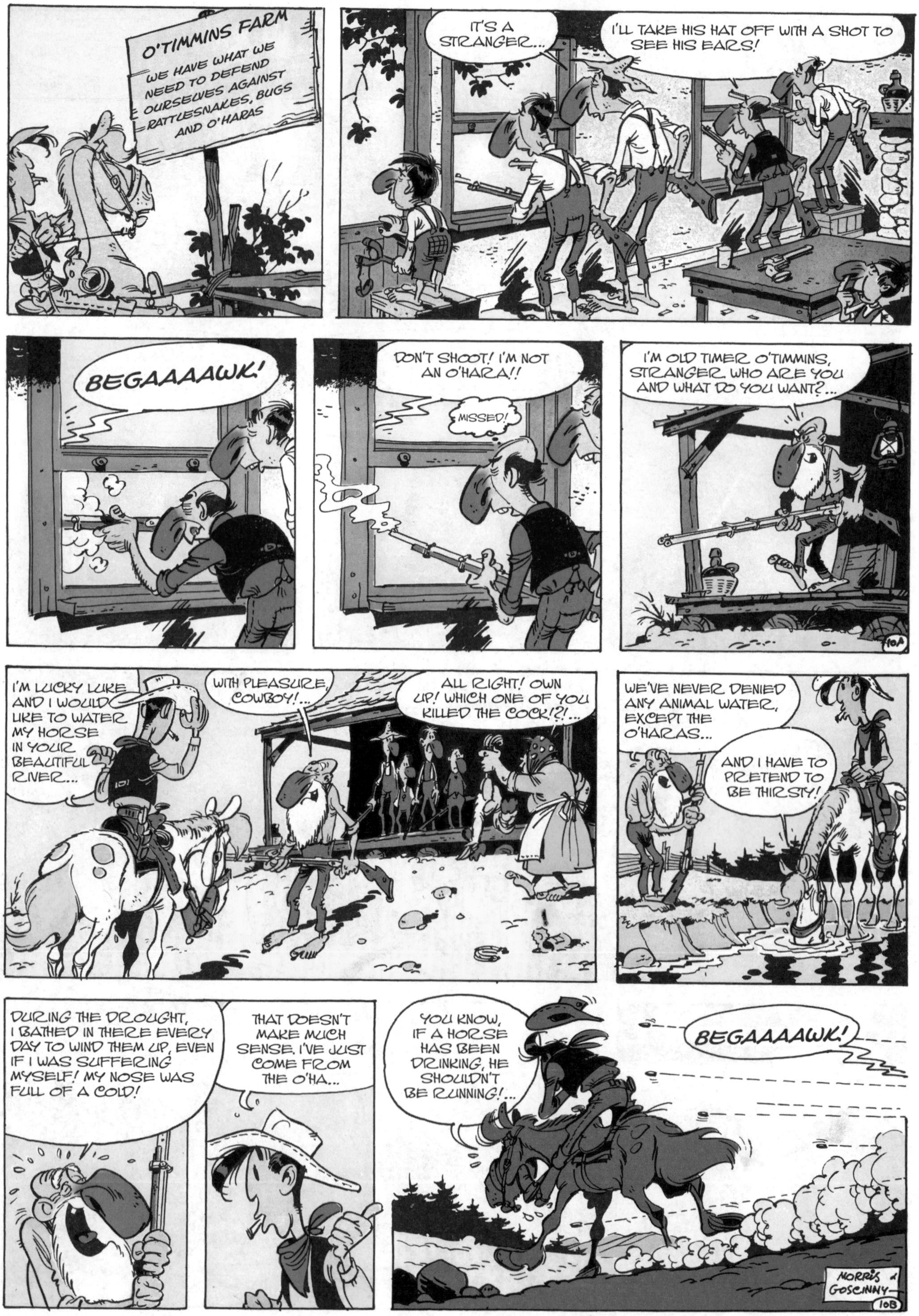

O'TIMMINS FARM
WE HAVE WHAT WE NEED TO DEFEND OURSELVES AGAINST RATTLESNAKES, BUGS AND O'HARAS
IT'S A STRANGER...
I'LL TAKE HIS HAT OFF WITH A SHOT TO SEE HIS EARS!
BEGAAAAWK!
DON'T SHOOT! I'M NOT AN O'HARA!!
MISSED!
I'M OLD TIMER O'TIMMINS, STRANGER. WHO ARE YOU AND WHAT DO YOU WANT?...
I'M LUCKY LUKE AND I WOULD LIKE TO WATER MY HORSE IN YOUR BEAUTIFUL RIVER...
WITH PLEASURE, COWBOY!...
ALL RIGHT! OWN UP! WHICH ONE OF YOU KILLED THE COCK!?!...
WE'VE NEVER DENIED ANY ANIMAL WATER, EXCEPT THE O'HARAS...
AND I HAVE TO PRETEND TO BE THIRSTY!
DURING THE DROUGHT, I BATHED IN THERE EVERY DAY TO WIND THEM UP, EVEN IF I WAS SUFFERING MYSELF! MY NOSE WAS FULL OF A COLD!
THAT DOESN'T MAKE MUCH SENSE. I'VE JUST COME FROM THE O'HA...
YOU KNOW, IF A HORSE HAS BEEN DRINKING, HE SHOULDN'T BE RUNNING!...
BEGAAAAWK!
MORRIS & GOSCINNY

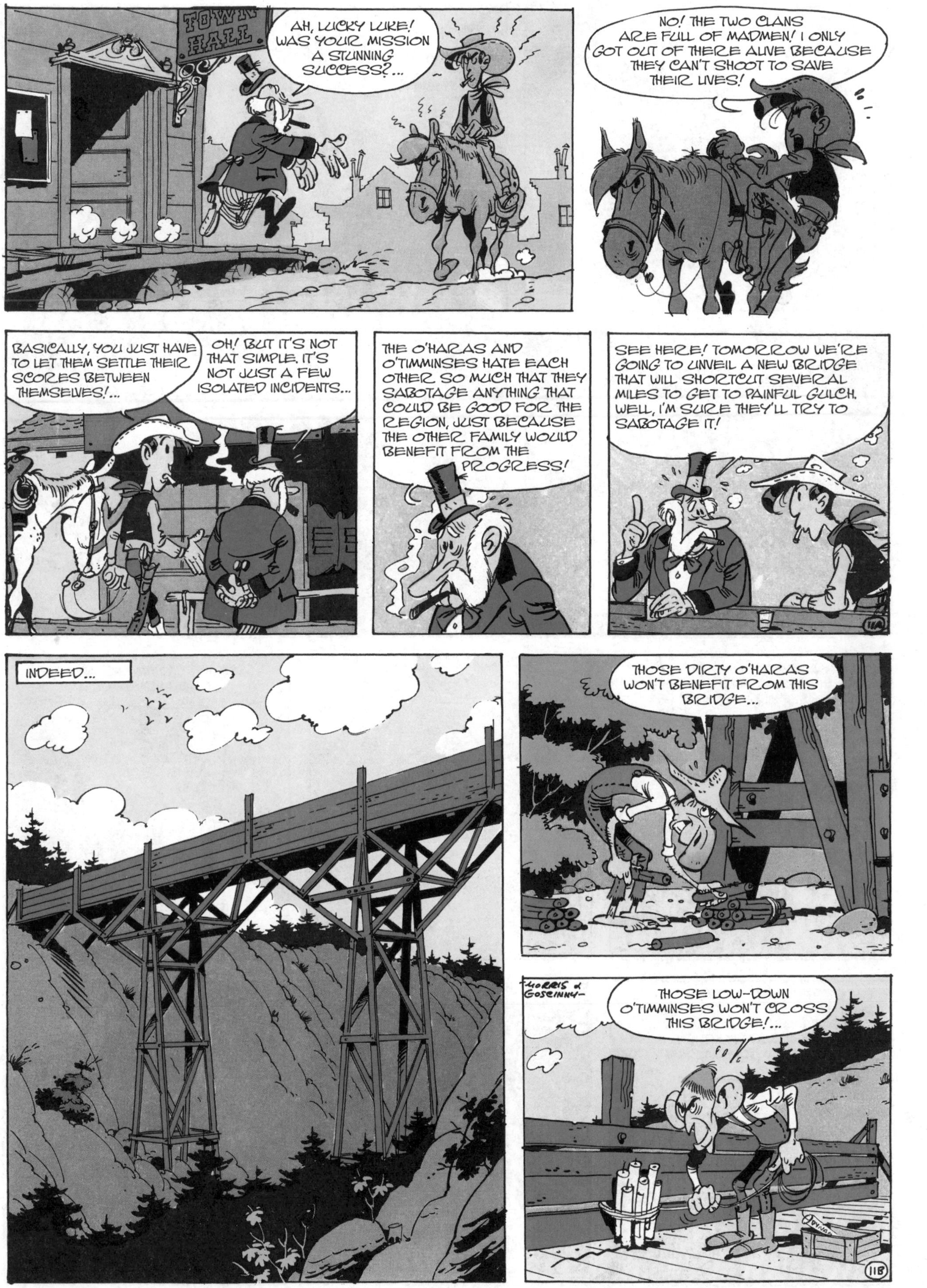
TOWN HALL
AH, LUCKY LUKE! WAS YOUR MISSION A STUNNING SUCCESS?...
NO! THE TWO CLANS ARE FULL OF MADMEN! I ONLY GOT OUT OF THERE ALIVE BECAUSE THEY CAN'T SHOOT TO SAVE THEIR LIVES!
BASICALLY, YOU JUST HAVE TO LET THEM SETTLE THEIR SCORES BETWEEN THEMSELVES!...
OH! BUT IT'S NOT THAT SIMPLE. IT'S NOT JUST A FEW ISOLATED INCIDENTS...
THE O'HARAS AND O'TIMMINSES HATE EACH OTHER SO MUCH THAT THEY SABOTAGE ANYTHING THAT COULD BE GOOD FOR THE REGION, JUST BECAUSE THE OTHER FAMILY WOULD BENEFIT FROM THE PROGRESS!
SEE HERE! TOMORROW WE'RE GOING TO UNVEIL A NEW BRIDGE THAT WILL SHORTCUT SEVERAL MILES TO GET TO PAINFUL GULCH. WELL, I'M SURE THEY'LL TRY TO SABOTAGE IT!
INDEED...
THOSE DIRTY O'HARAS WON'T BENEFIT FROM THIS BRIDGE...
MORRIS & GOSCINNY
THOSE LOW-DOWN O'TIMMINSES WON'T CROSS THIS BRIDGE!...

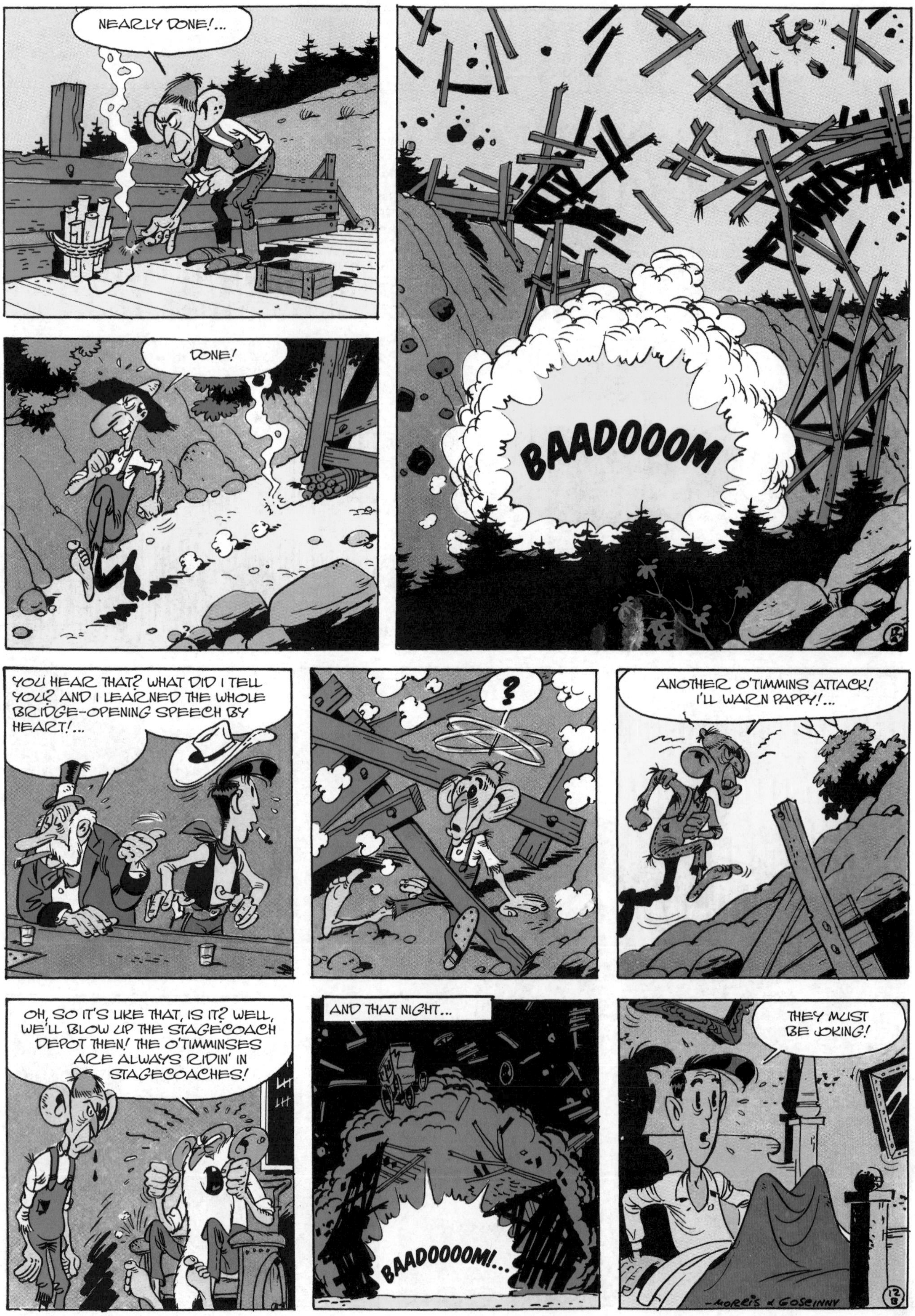
NEARLY DONE!...
DONE!
BAADOOOM
YOU HEAR THAT? WHAT DID I TELL YOU? AND I LEARNED THE WHOLE BRIDGE-OPENING SPEECH BY HEART!...
?
ANOTHER O'TIMMINS ATTACK! I'LL WARN PAPPY!...
OH, SO IT'S LIKE THAT, IS IT? WELL, WE'LL BLOW UP THE STAGECOACH DEPOT THEN! THE O'TIMMINSES ARE ALWAYS RIDIN' IN STAGECOACHES!
AND THAT NIGHT...
BAADOOOOM!...
THEY MUST BE JOKING!
MORRIS & GOSCINNY

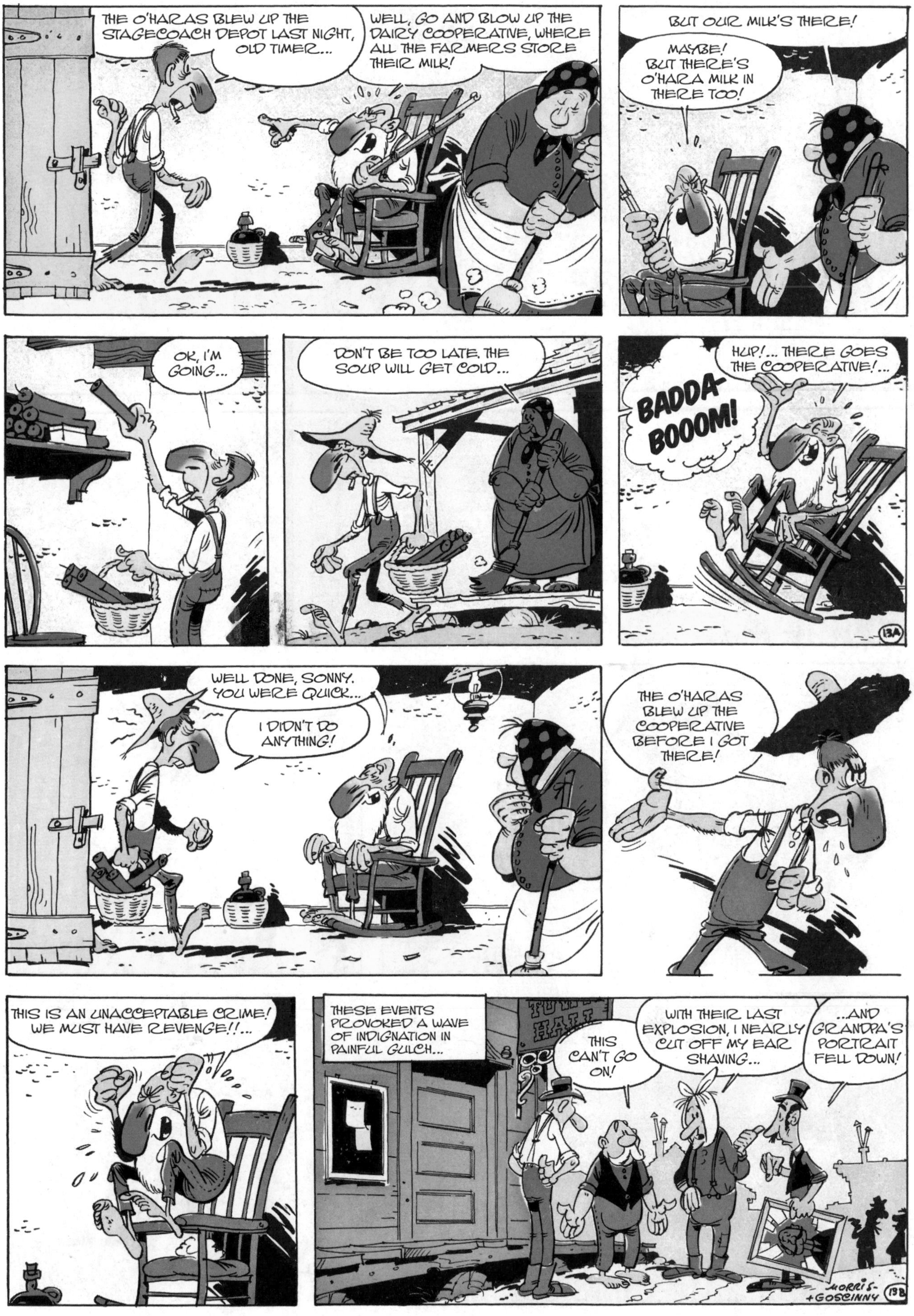
THE O'HARAS BLEW UP THE STAGECOACH DEPOT LAST NIGHT, OLD TIMER...
WELL, GO AND BLOW UP THE DAIRY COOPERATIVE, WHERE ALL THE FARMERS STORE THEIR MILK!
BUT OUR MILK'S THERE!
MAYBE! BUT THERE'S O'HARA MILK IN THERE TOO!
OK, I'M GOING...
DON'T BE TOO LATE. THE SOUP WILL GET COLD...
HUP!... THERE GOES THE COOPERATIVE!...
BADDA-BOOOM!
13A
WELL DONE, SONNY. YOU WERE QUICK...
I DIDN'T DO ANYTHING!
THE O'HARAS BLEW UP THE COOPERATIVE BEFORE I GOT THERE!
THIS IS AN UNACCEPTABLE CRIME! WE MUST HAVE REVENGE!!...
THESE EVENTS PROVOKED A WAVE OF INDIGNATION IN PAINFUL GULCH...
THIS CAN'T GO ON!
WITH THEIR LAST EXPLOSION, I NEARLY CUT OFF MY EAR SHAVING...
...AND GRANDPA'S PORTRAIT FELL DOWN!
MORRIS + GOSCINNY
13B

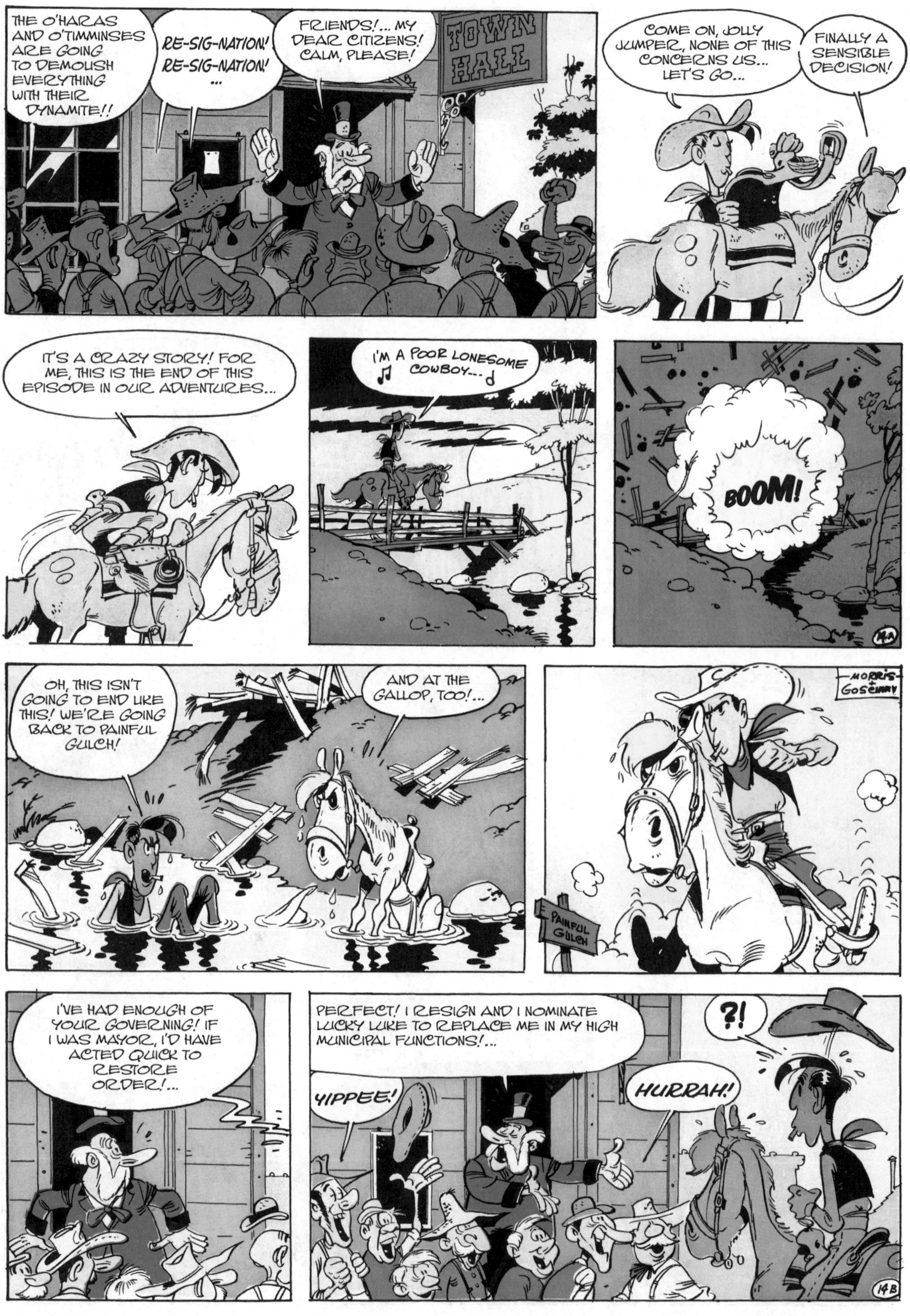
THE O'HARAS AND O'TIMMINSES ARE GOING TO DEMOLISH EVERYTHING WITH THEIR DYNAMITE!!
RE-SIG-NATION! RE-SIG-NATION! ...
FRIENDS!... MY DEAR CITIZENS! CALM, PLEASE!
TOWN HALL
COME ON, JOLLY JUMPER, NONE OF THIS CONCERNS US... LET'S GO...
FINALLY A SENSIBLE DECISION!
IT'S A CRAZY STORY! FOR ME, THIS IS THE END OF THIS EPISODE IN OUR ADVENTURES...
I'M A POOR LONESOME COWBOY...
BOOM!
OH, THIS ISN'T GOING TO END LIKE THIS! WE'RE GOING BACK TO PAINFUL GULCH!
AND AT THE GALLOP, TOO!...
MORRIS + GOSCINNY
PAINFUL GULCH
I'VE HAD ENOUGH OF YOUR GOVERNING! IF I WAS MAYOR, I'D HAVE ACTED QUICK TO RESTORE ORDER!...
PERFECT! I RESIGN AND I NOMINATE LUCKY LUKE TO REPLACE ME IN MY HIGH MUNICIPAL FUNCTIONS!...
?!
YIPPEE!
HURRAH!

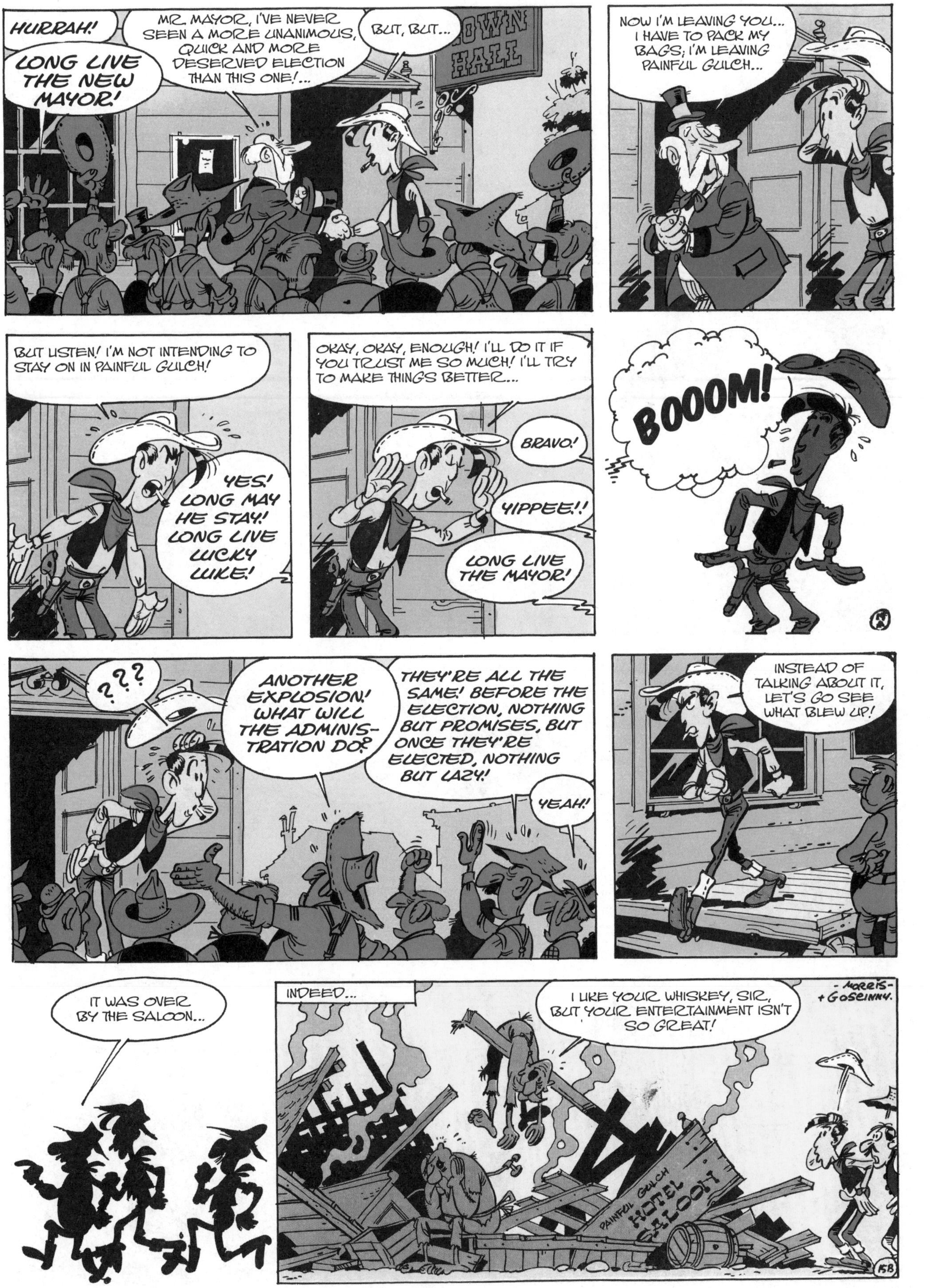
HURRAH!
LONG LIVE THE NEW MAYOR!
MR. MAYOR, I'VE NEVER SEEN A MORE UNANIMOUS, QUICK AND MORE DESERVED ELECTION THAN THIS ONE!...
BUT, BUT...
TOWN HALL
NOW I'M LEAVING YOU... I HAVE TO PACK MY BAGS; I'M LEAVING PAINFUL GULCH...
BUT LISTEN! I'M NOT INTENDING TO STAY ON IN PAINFUL GULCH!
YES! LONG MAY HE STAY! LONG LIVE LUCKY LUKE!
OKAY, OKAY, ENOUGH! I'LL DO IT IF YOU TRUST ME SO MUCH! I'LL TRY TO MAKE THINGS BETTER...
BRAVO!
YIPPEE!!
LONG LIVE THE MAYOR!
BOOOM!
???
ANOTHER EXPLOSION! WHAT WILL THE ADMINIS-TRATION DO?
THEY'RE ALL THE SAME! BEFORE THE ELECTION, NOTHING BUT PROMISES, BUT ONCE THEY'RE ELECTED, NOTHING BUT LAZY!
YEAH!
INSTEAD OF TALKING ABOUT IT, LET'S GO SEE WHAT BLEW UP!
IT WAS OVER BY THE SALOON...
INDEED...
I LIKE YOUR WHISKEY, SIR, BUT YOUR ENTERTAINMENT ISN'T SO GREAT!
- MORRIS - + GOSCINNY.
PAINFUL GULCH HOTEL SALOON

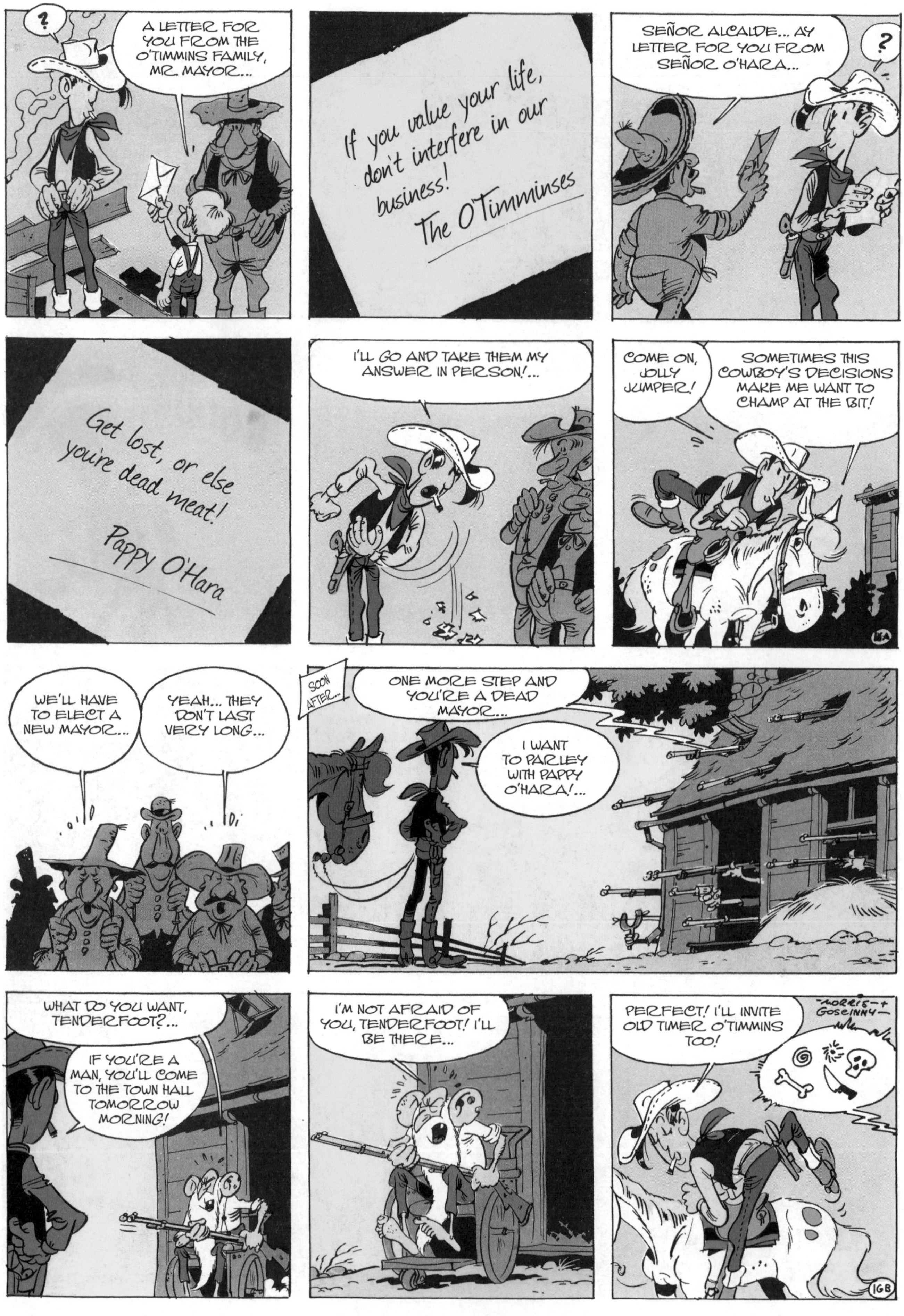
?
A LETTER FOR YOU FROM THE O'TIMMINS FAMILY, MR. MAYOR...
If you value your life, don't interfere in our business! The O'Timminses
SEÑOR ALCALDE... AY LETTER FOR YOU FROM SEÑOR O'HARA...
?
Get lost, or else you're dead meat! Pappy O'Hara
I'LL GO AND TAKE THEM MY ANSWER IN PERSON!...
COME ON, JOLLY JUMPER!
SOMETIMES THIS COWBOY'S DECISIONS MAKE ME WANT TO CHAMP AT THE BIT!
WE'LL HAVE TO ELECT A NEW MAYOR...
YEAH... THEY DON'T LAST VERY LONG...
SOON AFTER...
ONE MORE STEP AND YOU'RE A DEAD MAYOR...
I WANT TO PARLEY WITH PAPPY O'HARA!...
WHAT DO YOU WANT, TENDERFOOT?...
IF YOU'RE A MAN, YOU'LL COME TO THE TOWN HALL TOMORROW MORNING!
I'M NOT AFRAID OF YOU, TENDERFOOT! I'LL BE THERE...
PERFECT! I'LL INVITE OLD TIMER O'TIMMINS TOO!
MORRIS + GOSCINNY
16B

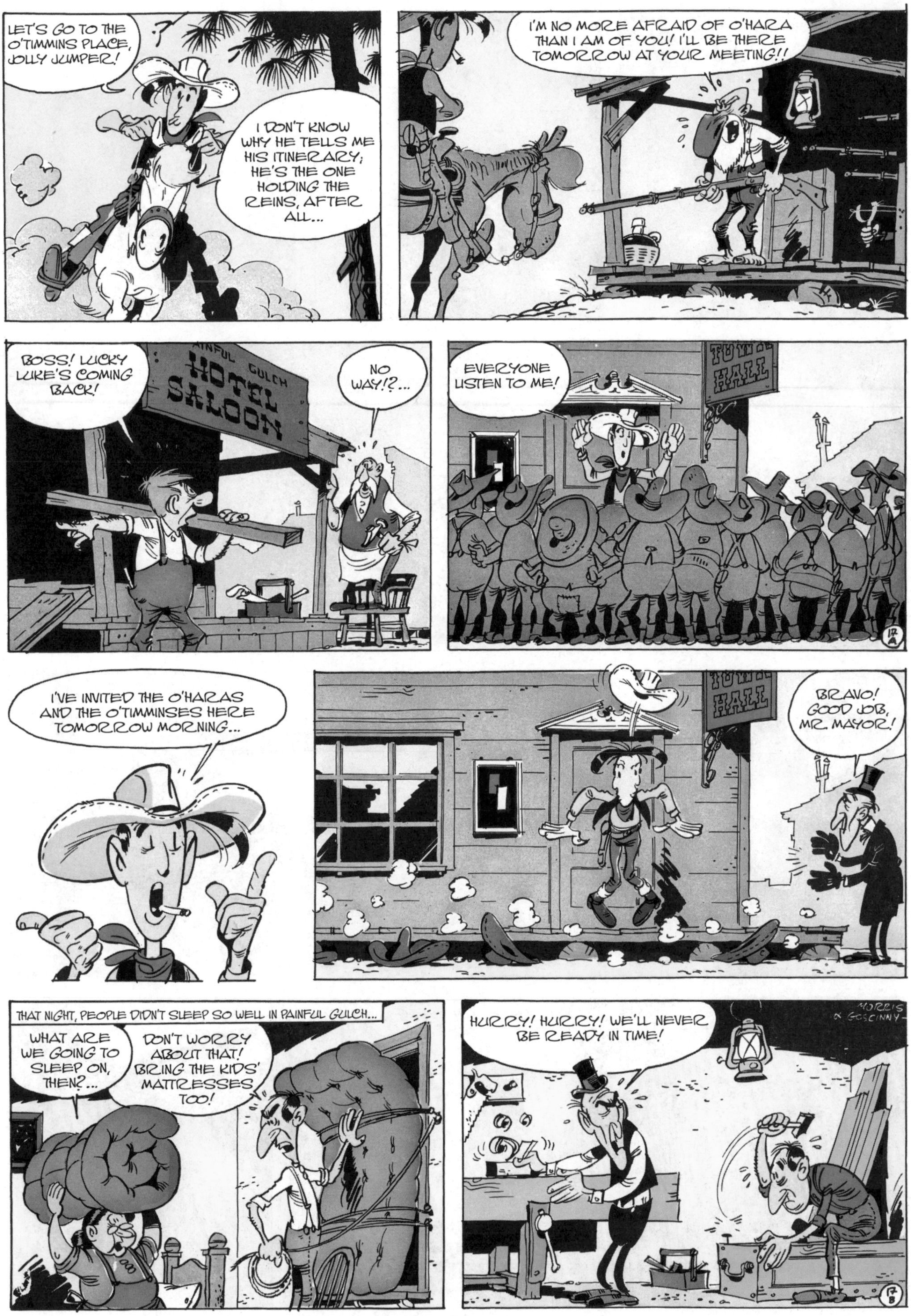
LET'S GO TO THE O'TIMMINS PLACE, JOLLY JUMPER!
I DON'T KNOW WHY HE TELLS ME HIS ITINERARY; HE'S THE ONE HOLDING THE REINS, AFTER ALL...
I'M NO MORE AFRAID OF O'HARA THAN I AM OF YOU! I'LL BE THERE TOMORROW AT YOUR MEETING!!
PAINFUL GULCH HOTEL SALOON
BOSS! LUCKY LUKE'S COMING BACK!
NO WAY!?...
TOWN HALL
EVERYONE LISTEN TO ME!
I'VE INVITED THE O'HARAS AND THE O'TIMMINSES HERE TOMORROW MORNING...
BRAVO! GOOD JOB, MR. MAYOR!
THAT NIGHT, PEOPLE DIDN'T SLEEP SO WELL IN PAINFUL GULCH...
WHAT ARE WE GOING TO SLEEP ON, THEN?...
DON'T WORRY ABOUT THAT! BRING THE KIDS' MATTRESSES TOO!
HURRY! HURRY! WE'LL NEVER BE READY IN TIME!
MORRIS & GOSCINNY

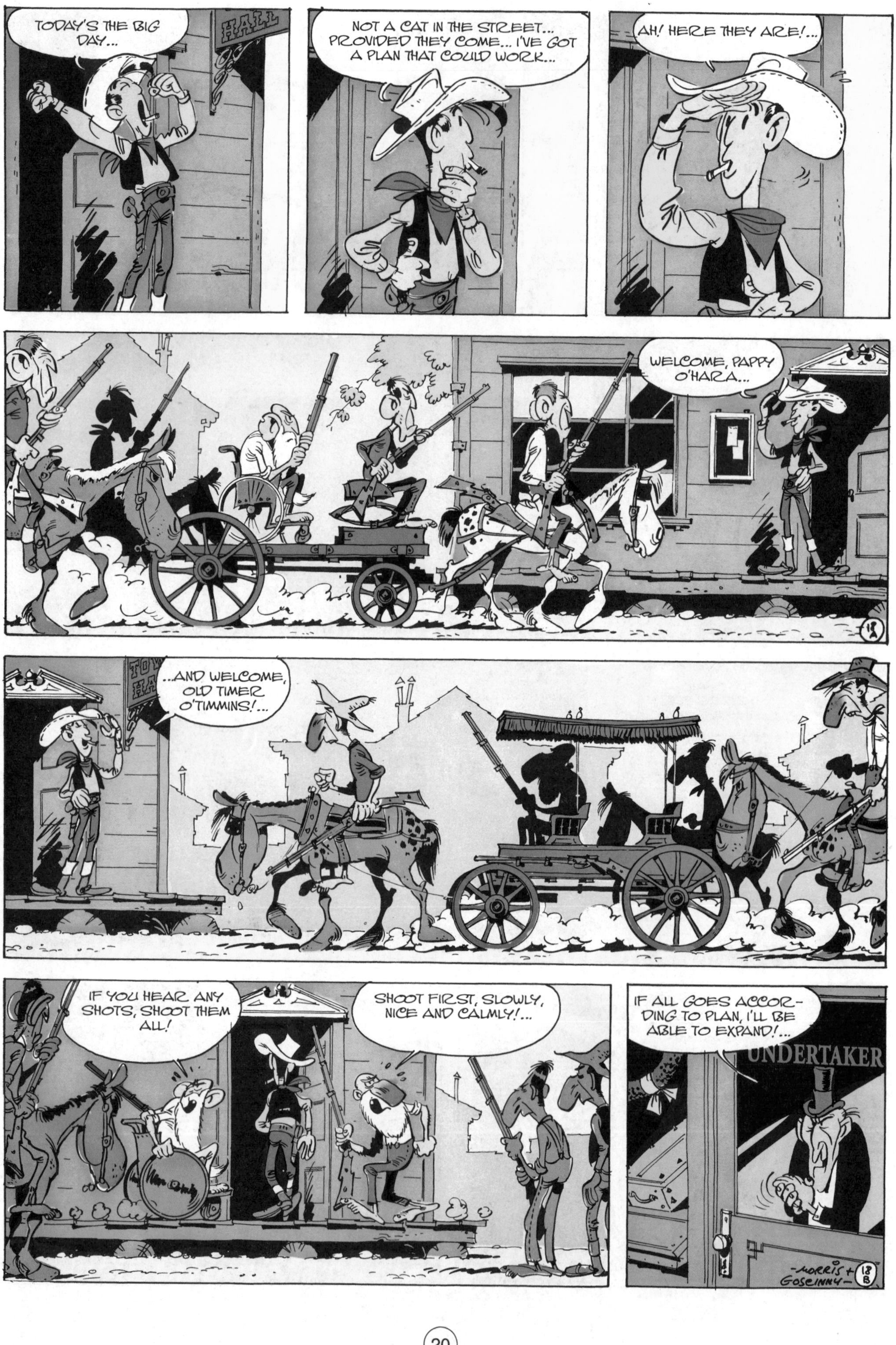
TODAY'S THE BIG DAY...
HALL
NOT A CAT IN THE STREET... PROVIDED THEY COME... I'VE GOT A PLAN THAT COULD WORK...
AH! HERE THEY ARE!...
WELCOME, PAPPY O'HARA...
...AND WELCOME, OLD TIMER O'TIMMINS!...
IF YOU HEAR ANY SHOTS, SHOOT THEM ALL!
SHOOT FIRST, SLOWLY, NICE AND CALMLY!...
IF ALL GOES ACCORDING TO PLAN, I'LL BE ABLE TO EXPAND!...
UNDERTAKER
MORRIS + GOSCINNY
18 B

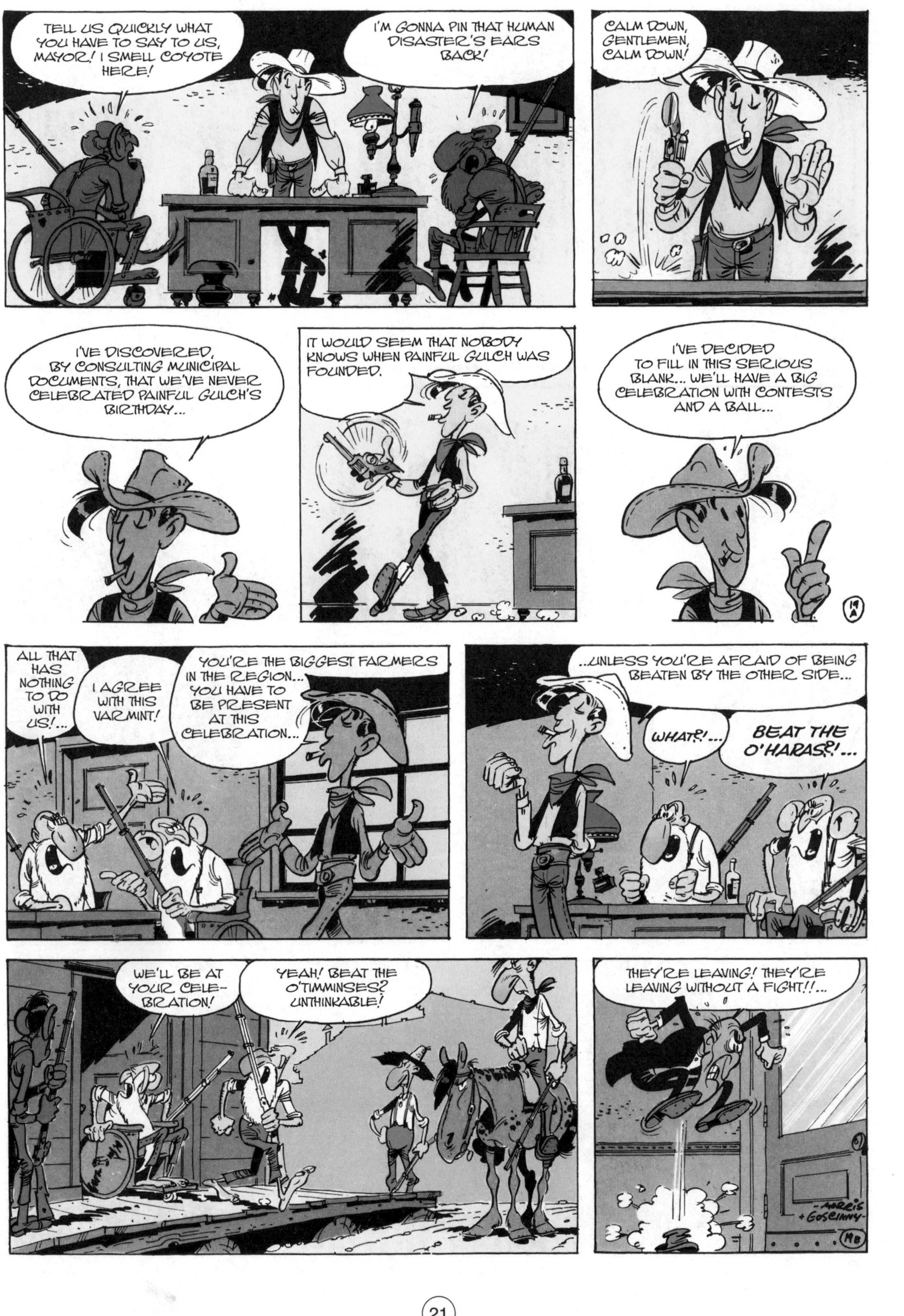
TELL US QUICKLY WHAT YOU HAVE TO SAY TO US, MAYOR! I SMELL COYOTE HERE!
I'M GONNA PIN THAT HUMAN DISASTER'S EARS BACK!
CALM DOWN, GENTLEMEN, CALM DOWN!
I'VE DISCOVERED, BY CONSULTING MUNICIPAL DOCUMENTS, THAT WE'VE NEVER CELEBRATED PAINFUL GULCH'S BIRTHDAY...
IT WOULD SEEM THAT NOBODY KNOWS WHEN PAINFUL GULCH WAS FOUNDED.
I'VE DECIDED TO FILL IN THIS SERIOUS BLANK... WE'LL HAVE A BIG CELEBRATION WITH CONTESTS AND A BALL...
ALL THAT HAS NOTHING TO DO WITH US!...
I AGREE WITH THIS VARMINT!
YOU'RE THE BIGGEST FARMERS IN THE REGION... YOU HAVE TO BE PRESENT AT THIS CELEBRATION...
...UNLESS YOU'RE AFRAID OF BEING BEATEN BY THE OTHER SIDE...
WHAT?!...
BEAT THE O'HARAS?!...
WE'LL BE AT YOUR CELE-BRATION!
YEAH! BEAT THE O'TIMMINSES? UNTHINKABLE!
THEY'RE LEAVING! THEY'RE LEAVING WITHOUT A FIGHT!!...
MORRIS + GOSCINNY

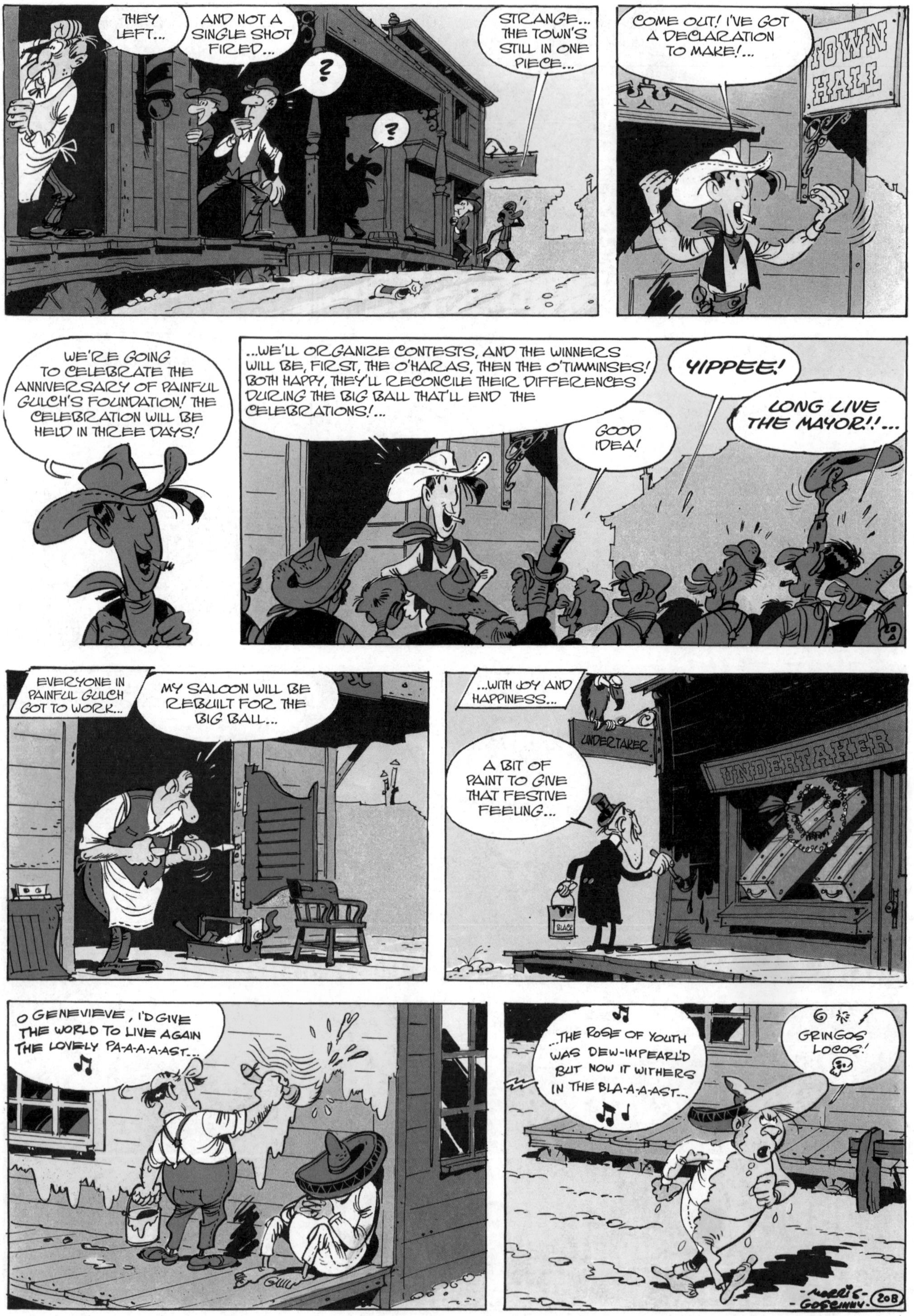

THEY LEFT...
AND NOT A SINGLE SHOT FIRED...
?
?
STRANGE... THE TOWN'S STILL IN ONE PIECE...
COME OUT! I'VE GOT A DECLARATION TO MAKE!...
TOWN HALL
WE'RE GOING TO CELEBRATE THE ANNIVERSARY OF PAINFUL GULCH'S FOUNDATION! THE CELEBRATION WILL BE HELD IN THREE DAYS!
...WE'LL ORGANIZE CONTESTS, AND THE WINNERS WILL BE, FIRST, THE O'HARAS, THEN THE O'TIMMINSES! BOTH HAPPY, THEY'LL RECONCILE THEIR DIFFERENCES DURING THE BIG BALL THAT'LL END THE CELEBRATIONS!...
GOOD IDEA!
YIPPEE!
LONG LIVE THE MAYOR!!...
EVERYONE IN PAINFUL GULCH GOT TO WORK...
MY SALOON WILL BE REBUILT FOR THE BIG BALL...
...WITH JOY AND HAPPINESS...
UNDERTAKER
UNDERTAKER
A BIT OF PAINT TO GIVE THAT FESTIVE FEELING...
BLACK
O GENEVIEVE, I'D GIVE THE WORLD TO LIVE AGAIN THE LOVELY PA-A-A-A-AST...
...THE ROSE OF YOUTH WAS DEW-IMPEARL'D BUT NOW IT WITHERS IN THE BLA-A-A-AST...
GRINGOS LOCOS!
-MORRIS- -GOSCINNY- 208

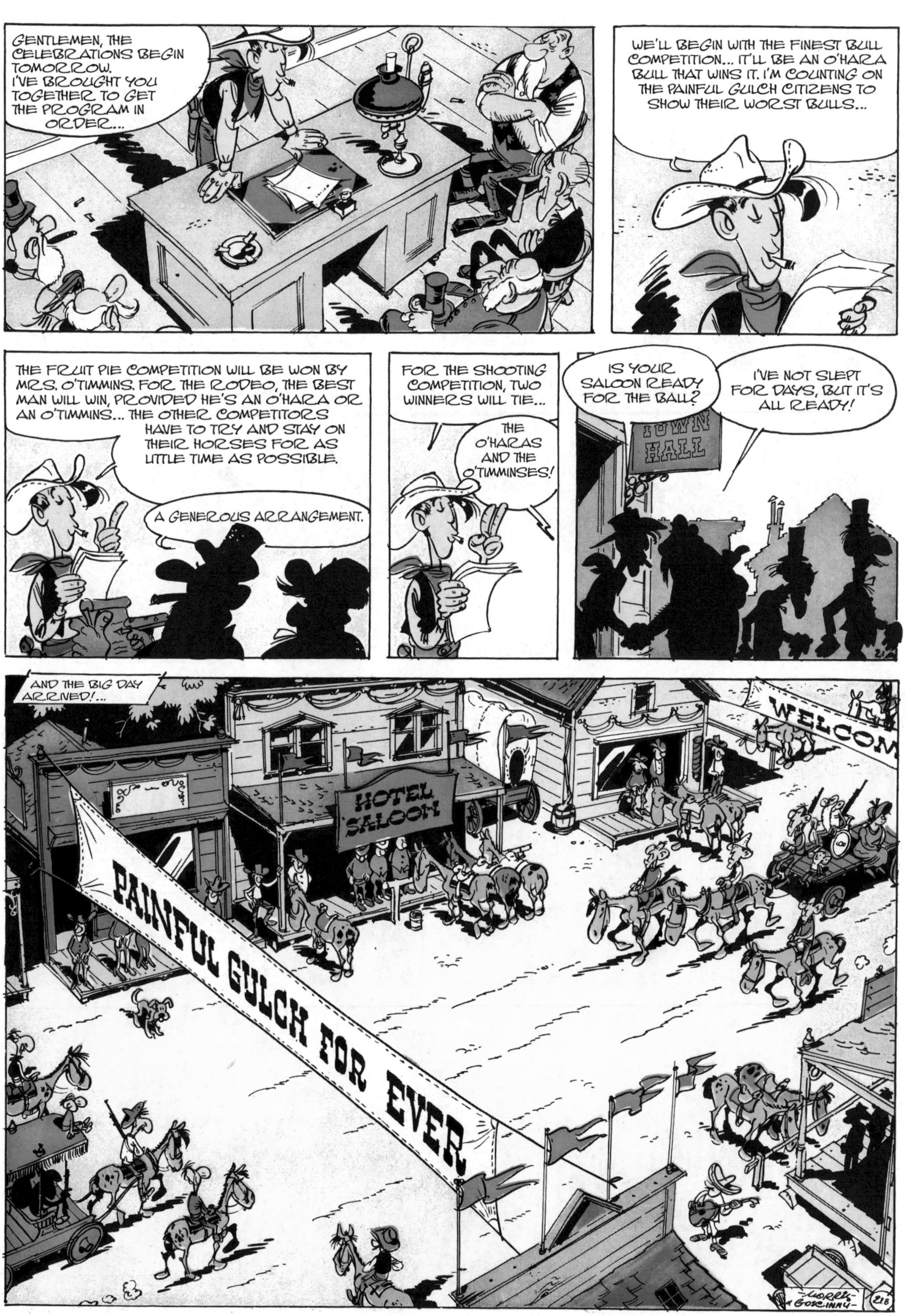
GENTLEMEN, THE CELEBRATIONS BEGIN TOMORROW. I'VE BROUGHT YOU TOGETHER TO GET THE PROGRAM IN ORDER...
WE'LL BEGIN WITH THE FINEST BULL COMPETITION... IT'LL BE AN O'HARA BULL THAT WINS IT. I'M COUNTING ON THE PAINFUL GULCH CITIZENS TO SHOW THEIR WORST BULLS...
THE FRUIT PIE COMPETITION WILL BE WON BY MRS. O'TIMMINS. FOR THE RODEO, THE BEST MAN WILL WIN, PROVIDED HE'S AN O'HARA OR AN O'TIMMINS... THE OTHER COMPETITORS HAVE TO TRY AND STAY ON THEIR HORSES FOR AS LITTLE TIME AS POSSIBLE.
A GENEROUS ARRANGEMENT.
FOR THE SHOOTING COMPETITION, TWO WINNERS WILL TIE...
THE O'HARAS AND THE O'TIMMINSES!
IS YOUR SALOON READY FOR THE BALL?
I'VE NOT SLEPT FOR DAYS, BUT IT'S ALL READY!
TOWN HALL
AND THE BIG DAY ARRIVED!...
HOTEL SALOON
WELCOM
PAINFUL GULCH FOR EVER

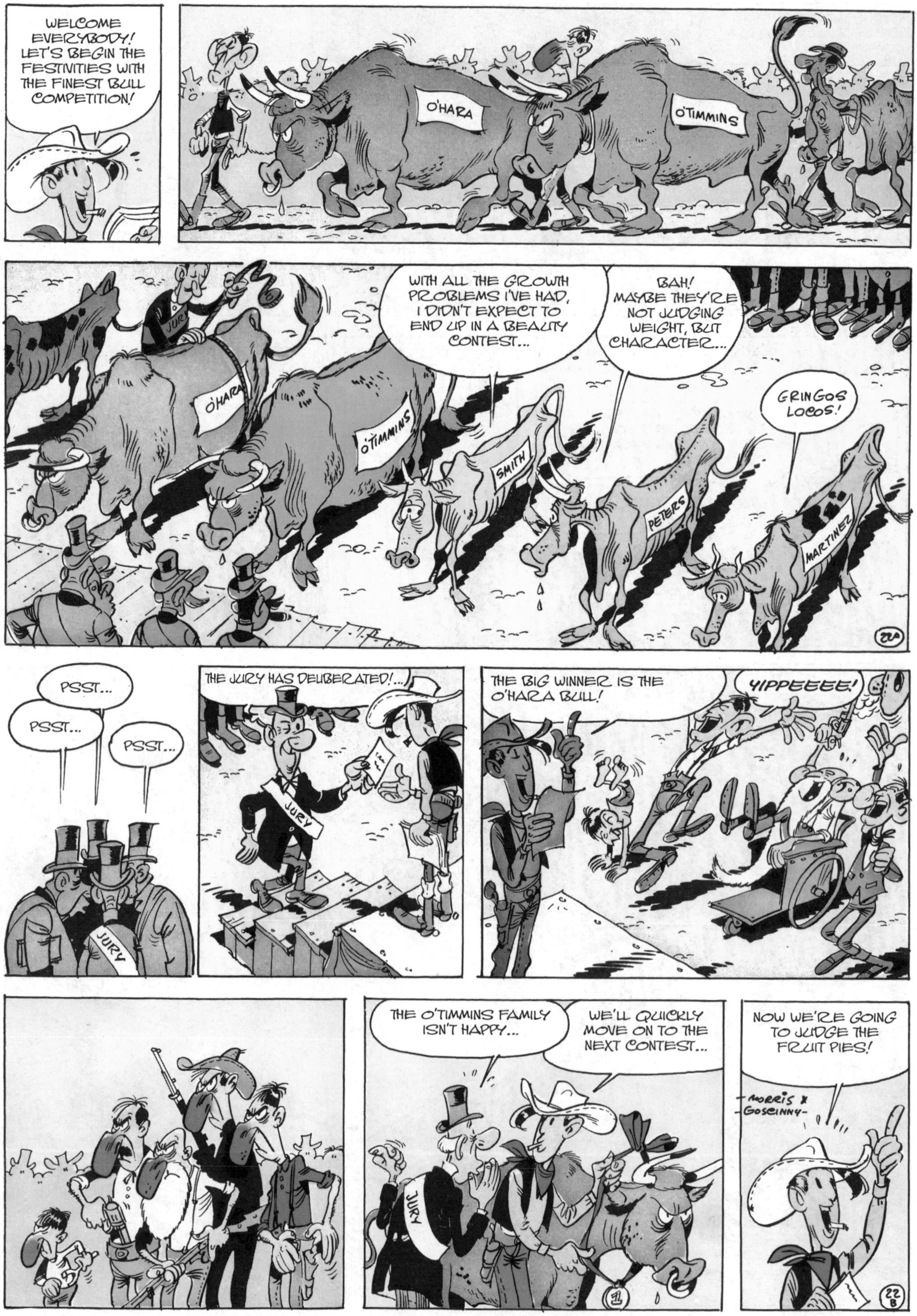
WELCOME EVERYBODY! LET'S BEGIN THE FESTIVITIES WITH THE FINEST BULL COMPETITION!
O'HARA
O'TIMMINS
JURY
O'HARA
O'TIMMINS
SMITH
PETERS
MARTINEZ
WITH ALL THE GROWTH PROBLEMS I'VE HAD, I DIDN'T EXPECT TO END UP IN A BEAUTY CONTEST...
BAH! MAYBE THEY'RE NOT JUDGING WEIGHT, BUT CHARACTER...
GRINGOS LOCOS!
22A
PSST...
PSST...
PSST...
JURY
THE JURY HAS DELIBERATED!...
JURY
THE BIG WINNER IS THE O'HARA BULL!
YIPPEEEEE!
THE O'TIMMINS FAMILY ISN'T HAPPY...
WE'LL QUICKLY MOVE ON TO THE NEXT CONTEST...
JURY
1
NOW WE'RE GOING TO JUDGE THE FRUIT PIES!
MORRIS & GOSCINNY
22B

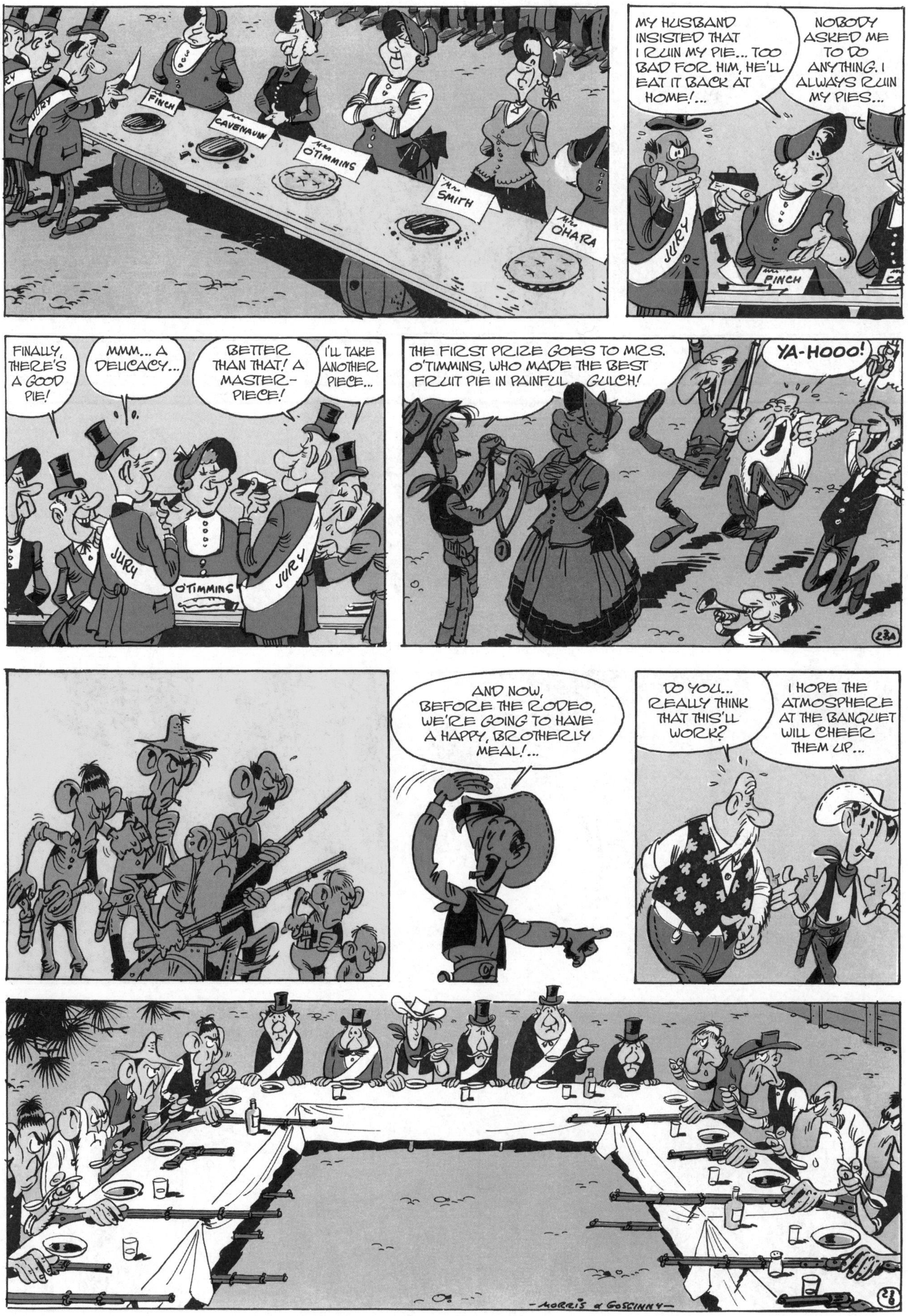
FINCH
MRS CAVENAUGH
MRS O'TIMMINS
MRS SMITH
MRS OHARA
MY HUSBAND INSISTED THAT I RUIN MY PIE... TOO BAD FOR HIM, HE'LL EAT IT BACK AT HOME!...
NOBODY ASKED ME TO DO ANYTHING. I ALWAYS RUIN MY PIES...
JURY
FINCH
FINALLY, THERE'S A GOOD PIE!
MMM... A DELICACY...
BETTER THAN THAT! A MASTER-PIECE!
I'LL TAKE ANOTHER PIECE...
JURY
O'TIMMINS
JURY
THE FIRST PRIZE GOES TO MRS. O'TIMMINS, WHO MADE THE BEST FRUIT PIE IN PAINFUL GULCH!
YA-HOOO!
AND NOW, BEFORE THE RODEO, WE'RE GOING TO HAVE A HAPPY, BROTHERLY MEAL!...
DO YOU... REALLY THINK THAT THIS'LL WORK?
I HOPE THE ATMOSPHERE AT THE BANQUET WILL CHEER THEM UP...
MORRIS & GOSCINNY

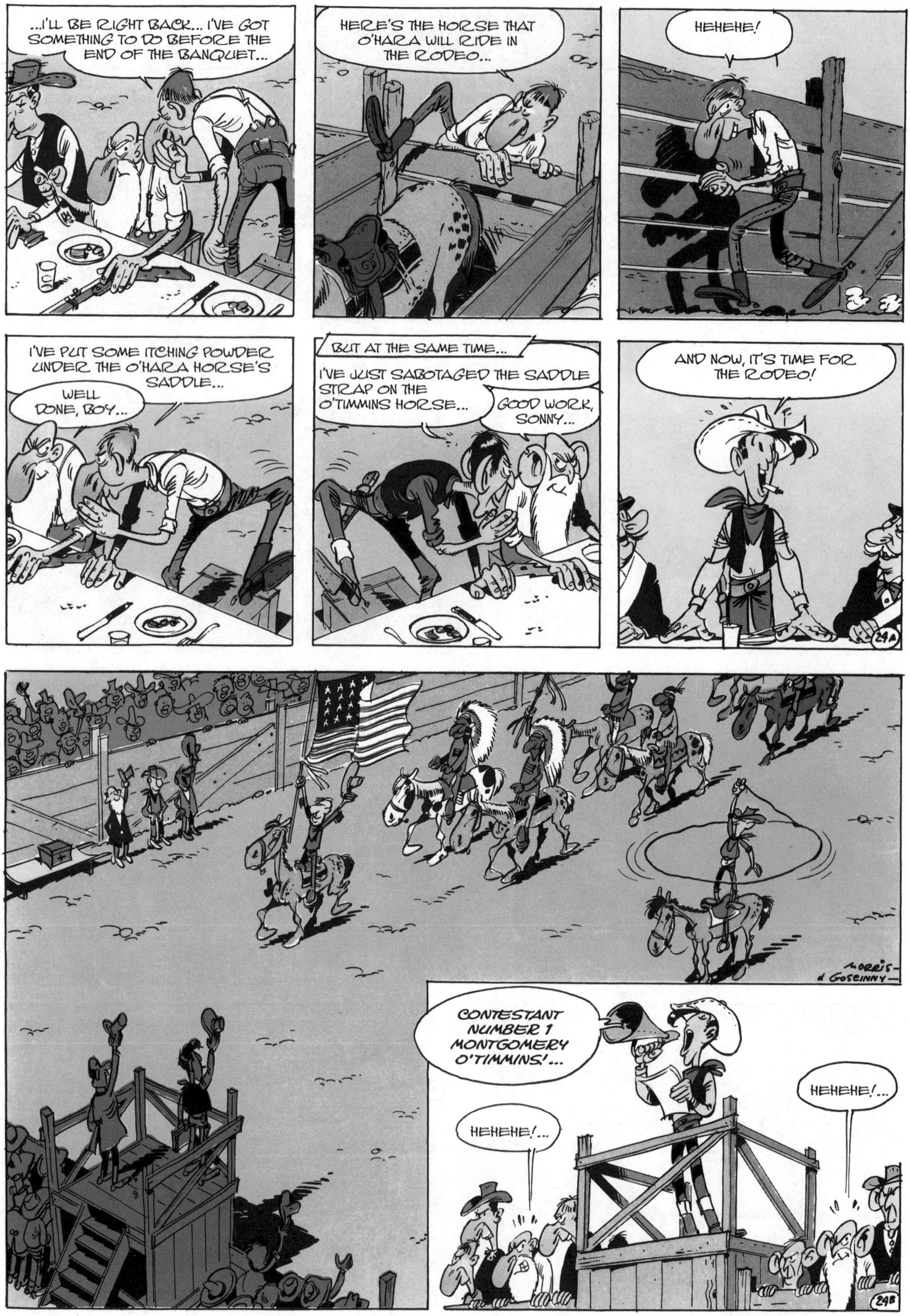
...I'LL BE RIGHT BACK... I'VE GOT SOMETHING TO DO BEFORE THE END OF THE BANQUET...
HERE'S THE HORSE THAT O'HARA WILL RIDE IN THE RODEO...
HEHEHE!
I'VE PUT SOME ITCHING POWDER UNDER THE O'HARA HORSE'S SADDLE...
WELL DONE, BOY...
BUT AT THE SAME TIME...
I'VE JUST SABOTAGED THE SADDLE STRAP ON THE O'TIMMINS HORSE...
GOOD WORK, SONNY...
AND NOW, IT'S TIME FOR THE RODEO!
24A
MORRIS
& GOSCINNY
CONTESTANT NUMBER 1 MONTGOMERY O'TIMMINS!...
HEHEHE!...
HEHEHE!...
24B

OPEN THE GATE!...

SNAP!

TIME: 4 SECONDS!

OK!

CONTESTANT NUMBER 2: NATHANIEL O'HARA!

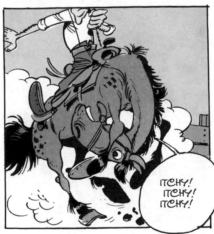

ITCHY! ITCHY! ITCHY!

TIME: 4 SECONDS!

SPLAFF

IF I EVER FIND OUT WHO PLAYED THIS CHILDISH PRANK, I'LL GIVE HIM THE WORST HOOFING OF HIS LIFE!

...YOU KNOW THE DRILL, NONE OF YOU CAN STAY IN THE SADDLE FOR MORE THAN THREE SECONDS...

— MORRIS & GOSCINNY —

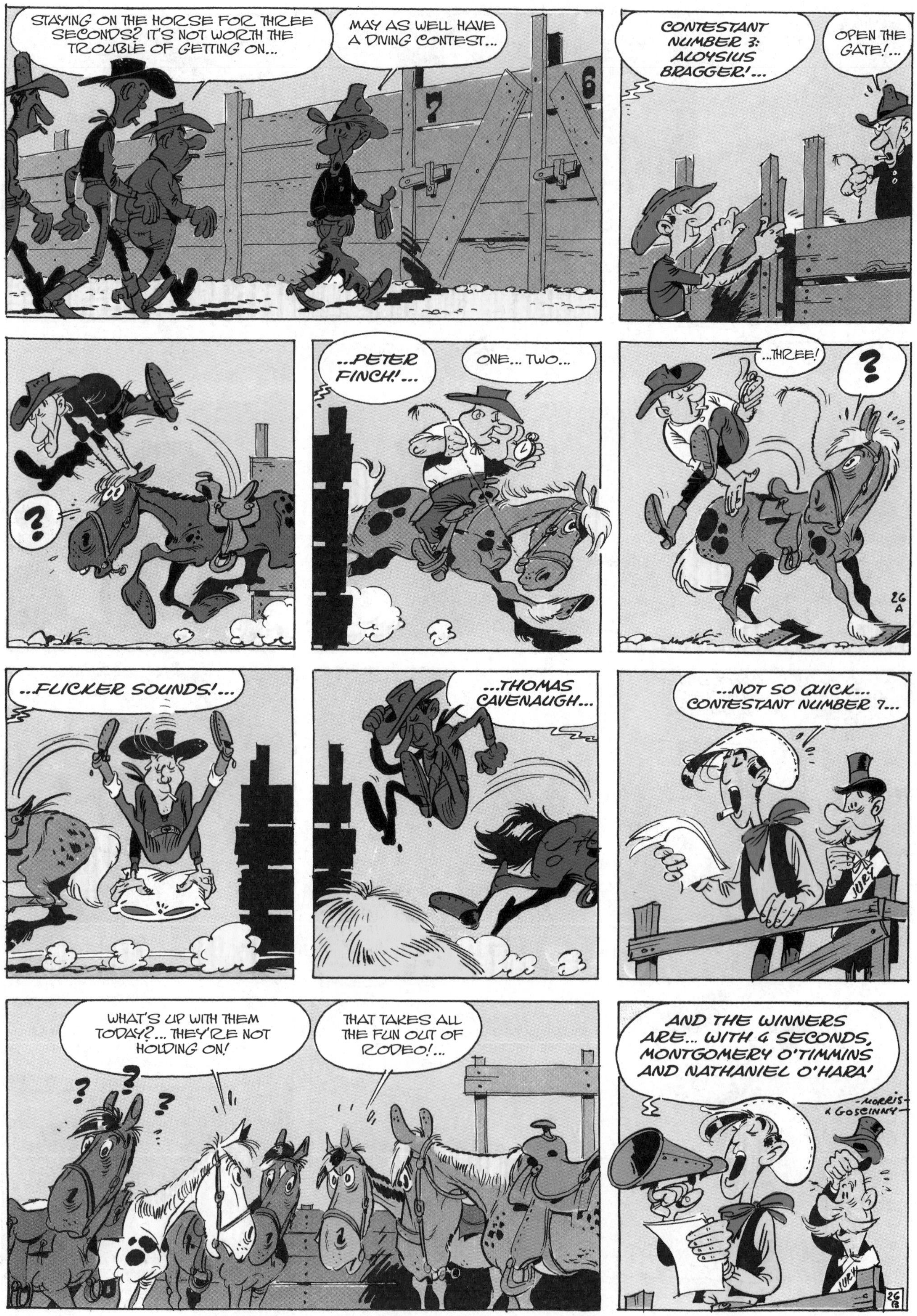
STAYING ON THE HORSE FOR THREE SECONDS? IT'S NOT WORTH THE TROUBLE OF GETTING ON...
MAY AS WELL HAVE A DIVING CONTEST...
CONTESTANT NUMBER 3: ALOYSIUS BRAGGER! ...
OPEN THE GATE! ...
?
...PETER FINCH! ...
ONE... TWO...
...THREE!
?
26 A
...FLICKER SOUNDS! ...
...THOMAS CAVENAUGH...
...NOT SO QUICK... CONTESTANT NUMBER 7...
JURY
WHAT'S UP WITH THEM TODAY?... THEY'RE NOT HOLDING ON!
THAT TAKES ALL THE FUN OUT OF RODEO! ...
? ? ?
AND THE WINNERS ARE... WITH 4 SECONDS, MONTGOMERY O'TIMMINS AND NATHANIEL O'HARA!
-MORRIS- & GOSCINNY-
JURY
26 B

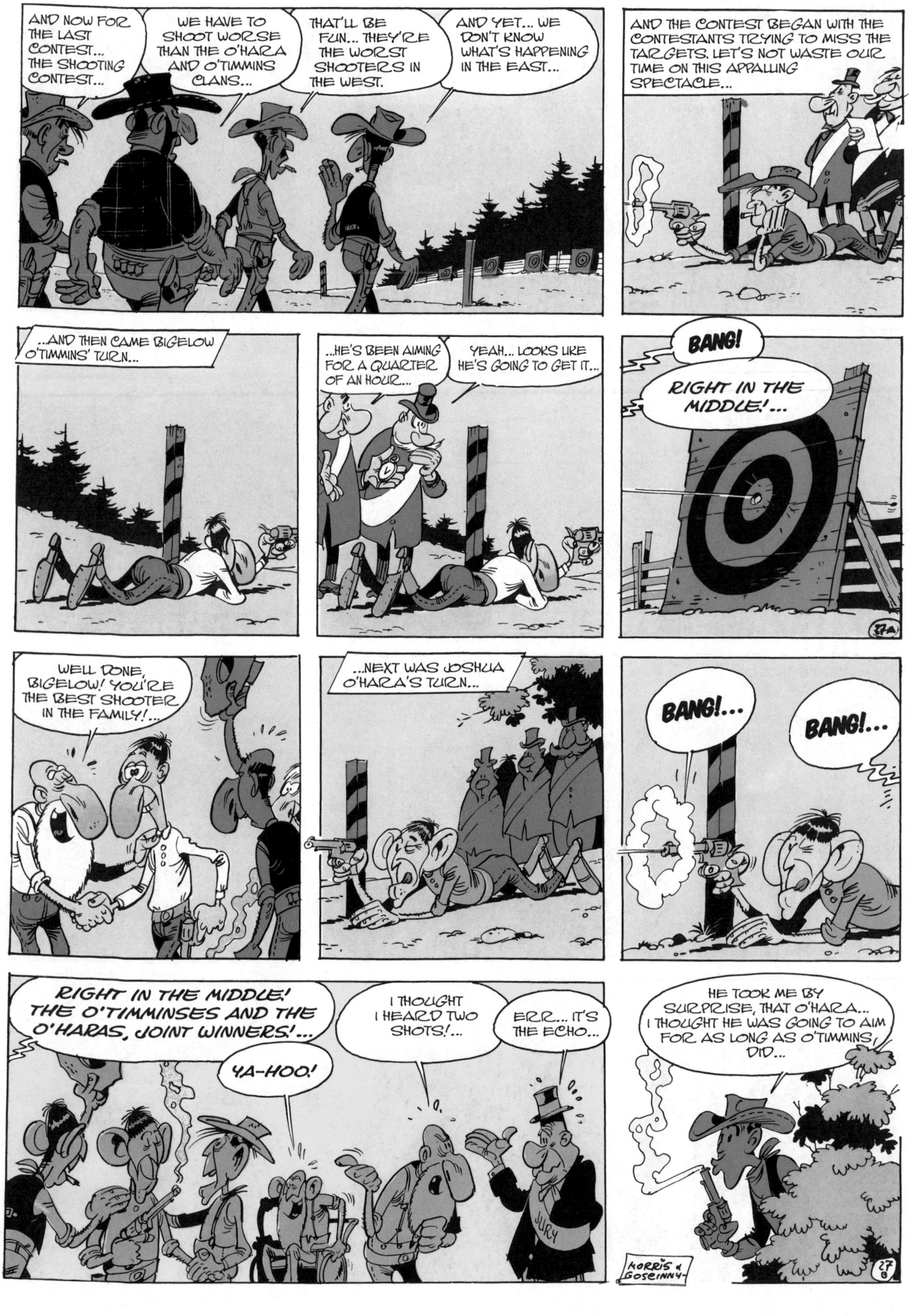

AND NOW FOR THE LAST CONTEST... THE SHOOTING CONTEST...
WE HAVE TO SHOOT WORSE THAN THE O'HARA AND O'TIMMINS CLANS...
THAT'LL BE FUN... THEY'RE THE WORST SHOOTERS IN THE WEST.
AND YET... WE DON'T KNOW WHAT'S HAPPENING IN THE EAST...
AND THE CONTEST BEGAN WITH THE CONTESTANTS TRYING TO MISS THE TARGETS. LET'S NOT WASTE OUR TIME ON THIS APPALLING SPECTACLE...
...AND THEN CAME BIGELOW O'TIMMINS' TURN...
...HE'S BEEN AIMING FOR A QUARTER OF AN HOUR...
YEAH... LOOKS LIKE HE'S GOING TO GET IT...
BANG!
RIGHT IN THE MIDDLE!...
WELL DONE, BIGELOW! YOU'RE THE BEST SHOOTER IN THE FAMILY!...
...NEXT WAS JOSHUA O'HARA'S TURN...
BANG!...
BANG!...
RIGHT IN THE MIDDLE! THE O'TIMMINSES AND THE O'HARAS, JOINT WINNERS!...
YA-HOO!
I THOUGHT I HEARD TWO SHOTS!...
ERR... IT'S THE ECHO...
JURY
HE TOOK ME BY SURPRISE, THAT O'HARA... I THOUGHT HE WAS GOING TO AIM FOR AS LONG AS O'TIMMINS DID...
MORRIS & GOSCINNY

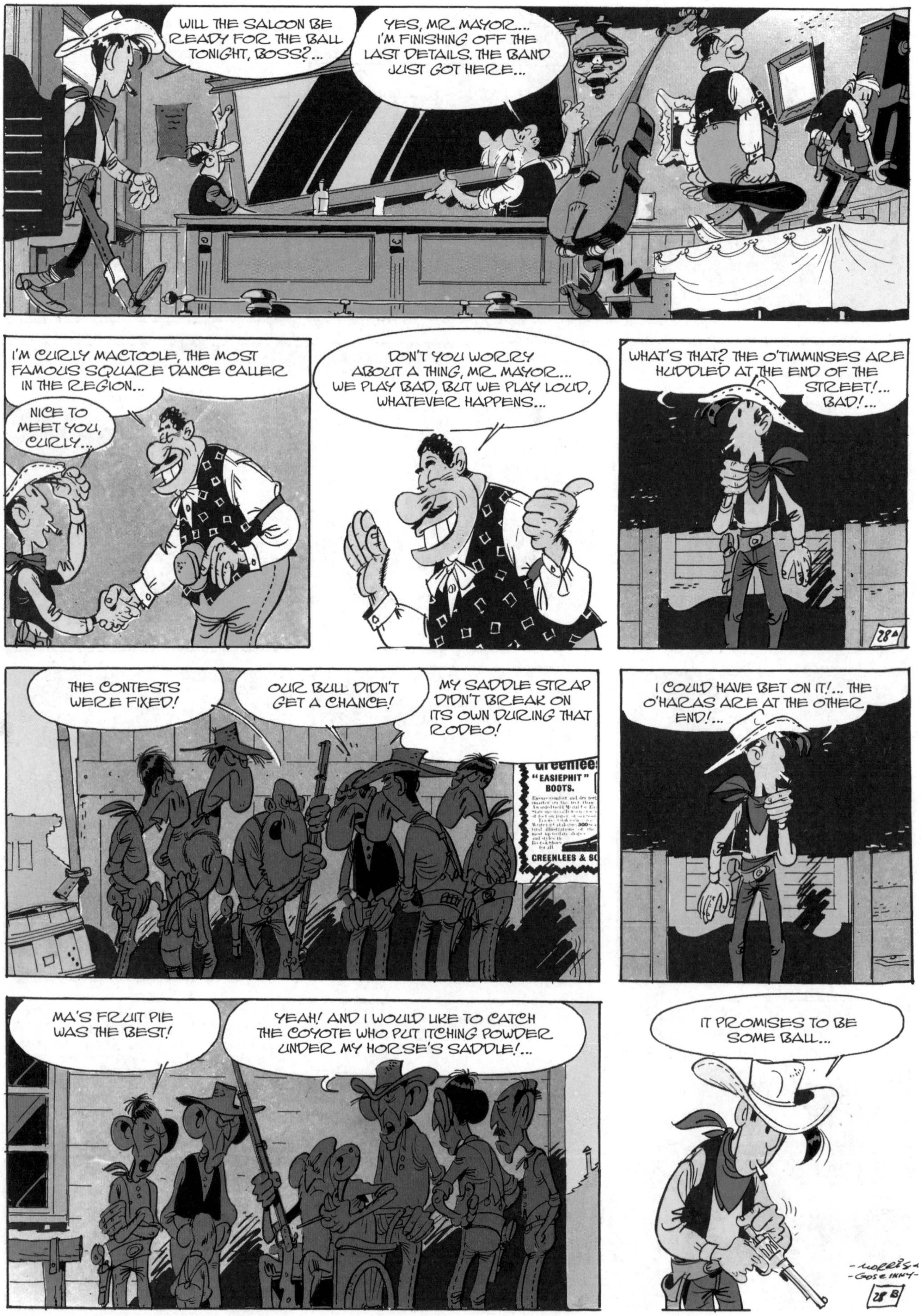
WILL THE SALOON BE READY FOR THE BALL TONIGHT, BOSS?...
YES, MR. MAYOR... I'M FINISHING OFF THE LAST DETAILS. THE BAND JUST GOT HERE...
I'M CURLY MACTOOLE, THE MOST FAMOUS SQUARE DANCE CALLER IN THE REGION...
NICE TO MEET YOU, CURLY...
DON'T YOU WORRY ABOUT A THING, MR. MAYOR... WE PLAY BAD, BUT WE PLAY LOUD, WHATEVER HAPPENS...
WHAT'S THAT? THE O'TIMMINSES ARE HUDDLED AT THE END OF THE STREET!... BAD!...
28A
THE CONTESTS WERE FIXED!
OUR BULL DIDN'T GET A CHANCE!
MY SADDLE STRAP DIDN'T BREAK ON ITS OWN DURING THAT RODEO!
"EASIEPHIT" BOOTS.
GREENLEES & SO
I COULD HAVE BET ON IT!... THE O'HARAS ARE AT THE OTHER END!...
MA'S FRUIT PIE WAS THE BEST!
YEAH! AND I WOULD LIKE TO CATCH THE COYOTE WHO PUT ITCHING POWDER UNDER MY HORSE'S SADDLE!...
IT PROMISES TO BE SOME BALL...
MORRIS & GOSCINNY
28B

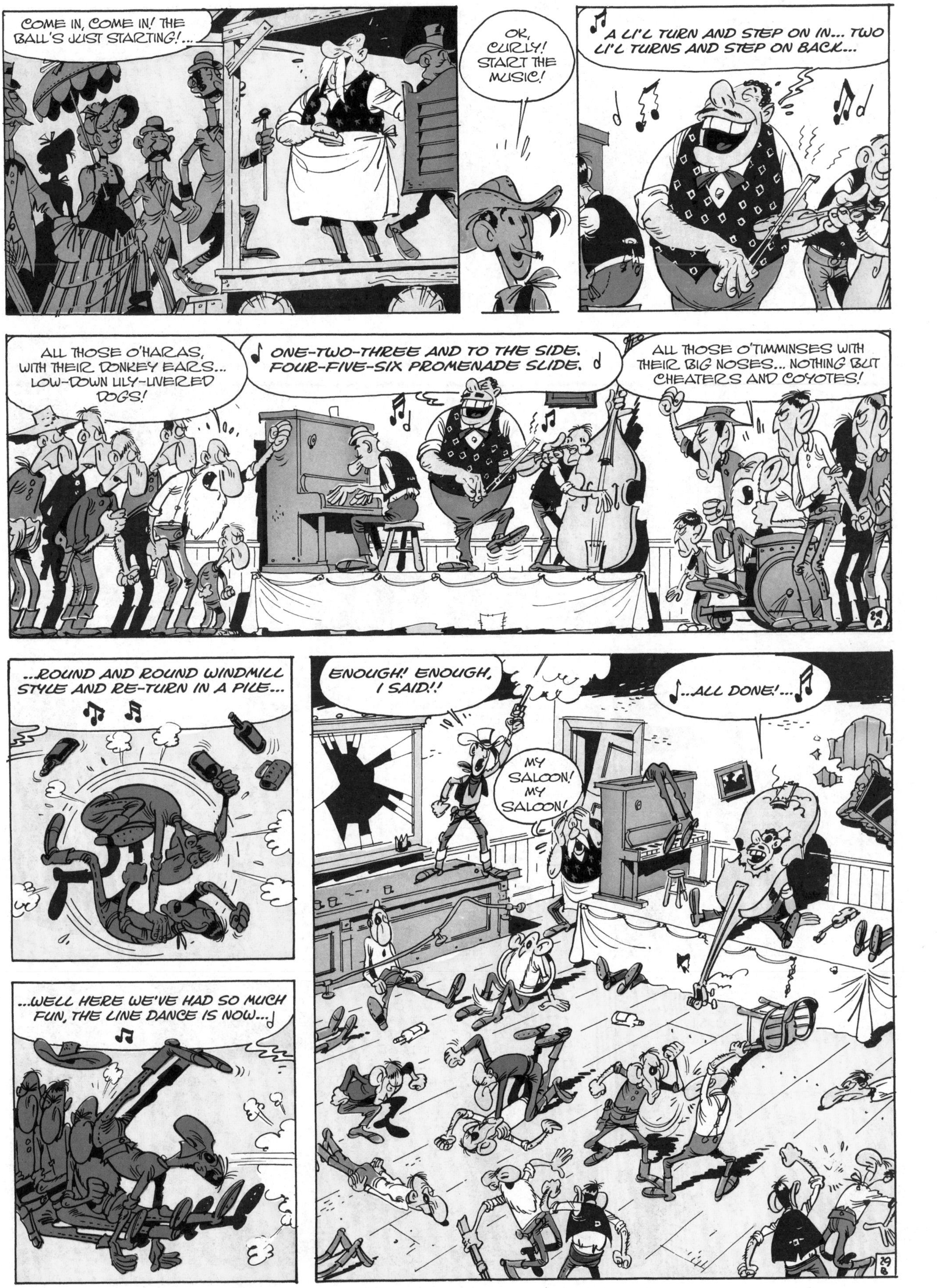
COME IN, COME IN! THE BALL'S JUST STARTING!...
OK, CURLY! START THE MUSIC!
A LI'L TURN AND STEP ON IN... TWO LI'L TURNS AND STEP ON BACK...
ALL THOSE O'HARAS, WITH THEIR DONKEY EARS... LOW-DOWN LILY-LIVERED DOGS!
ONE-TWO-THREE AND TO THE SIDE. FOUR-FIVE-SIX PROMENADE SLIDE.
ALL THOSE O'TIMMINSES WITH THEIR BIG NOSES... NOTHING BUT CHEATERS AND COYOTES!
...ROUND AND ROUND WINDMILL STYLE AND RE-TURN IN A PILE...
...WELL HERE WE'VE HAD SO MUCH FUN, THE LINE DANCE IS NOW...
ENOUGH! ENOUGH, I SAID!!
...ALL DONE!...
MY SALOON! MY SALOON!

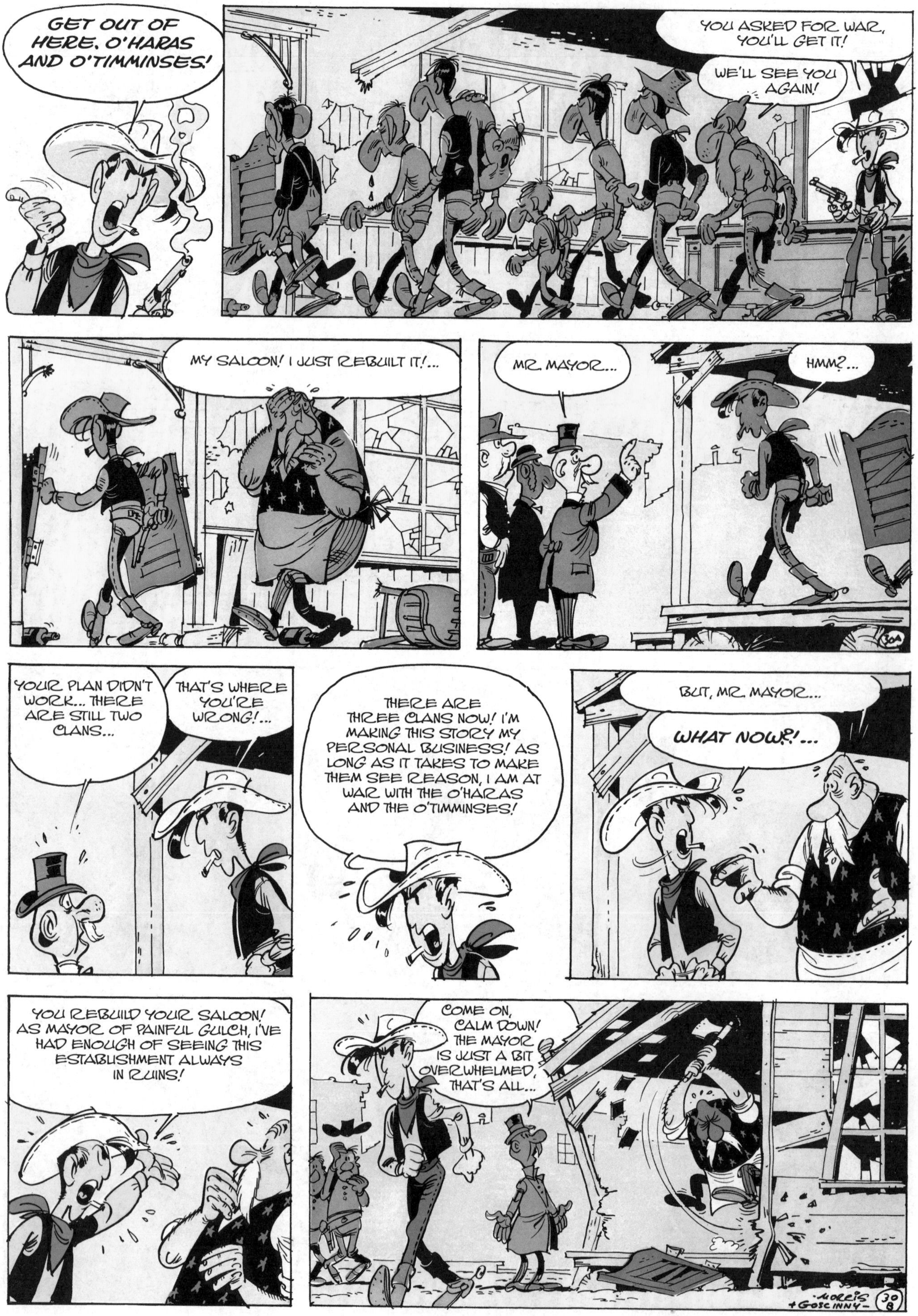

GET OUT OF HERE, O'HARAS AND O'TIMMINSES!
YOU ASKED FOR WAR, YOU'LL GET IT!
WE'LL SEE YOU AGAIN!
MY SALOON! I JUST REBUILT IT!...
MR. MAYOR...
HMM?...
YOUR PLAN DIDN'T WORK... THERE ARE STILL TWO CLANS...
THAT'S WHERE YOU'RE WRONG!...
THERE ARE THREE CLANS NOW! I'M MAKING THIS STORY MY PERSONAL BUSINESS! AS LONG AS IT TAKES TO MAKE THEM SEE REASON, I AM AT WAR WITH THE O'HARAS AND THE O'TIMMINSES!
BUT, MR. MAYOR...
WHAT NOW?!...
YOU REBUILD YOUR SALOON! AS MAYOR OF PAINFUL GULCH, I'VE HAD ENOUGH OF SEEING THIS ESTABLISHMENT ALWAYS IN RUINS!
COME ON, CALM DOWN! THE MAYOR IS JUST A BIT OVERWHELMED, THAT'S ALL...
MORRIS + GOSCINNY
30 B

A TRAP! I NEED TO SPRING A TRAP... AND I HAVE AN IDEA...

JUST WHAT I NEED!

I'LL BUY YOUR HAY FOR ANY AMOUNT YOU SAY...

THAT'S EXACTLY MY PRICE...

YOU'RE GOING TO MAKE ME A HUT, BY THE TREE OVER THERE...

?

CRAZY! HE'S CRAZY!

PERFECT! NOW DISAPPEAR!

I'VE NO INTENTION OF HANGING AROUND...

NOW I JUST HAVE TO WAIT FOR A FISH TO TAKE THE BAIT...

O'HARA PROPERTY

Hands off, O'Timminses!

LOOK! I HAVE TO GO AND TELL THE O'TIMMINS CLAN... THEY'LL SLIP ME SOME MONEY...

O'HARA PROPERTY

Hands off, O'Timminses!

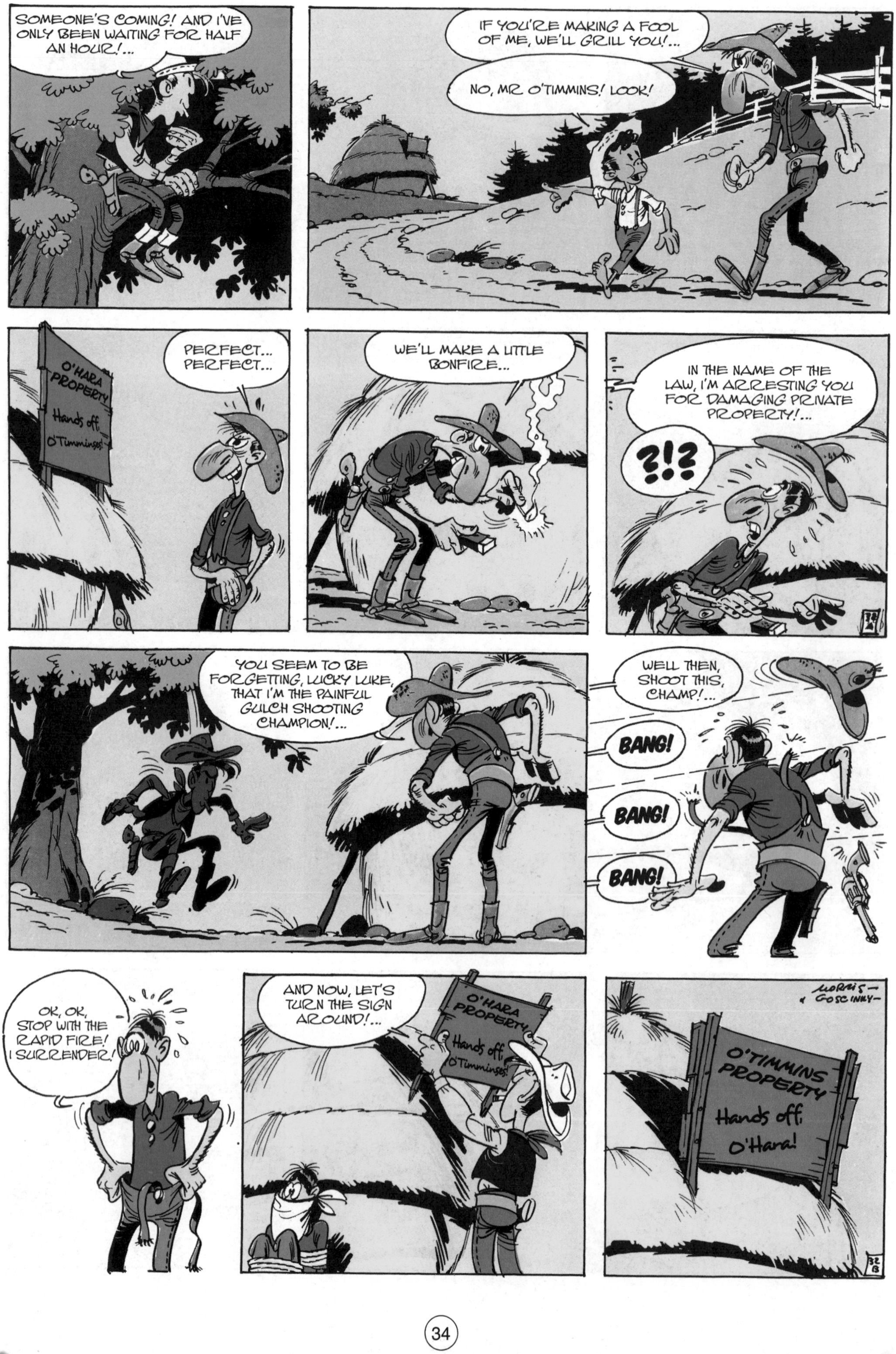
SOMEONE'S COMING! AND I'VE ONLY BEEN WAITING FOR HALF AN HOUR!...
IF YOU'RE MAKING A FOOL OF ME, WE'LL GRILL YOU!...
NO, MR O'TIMMINS! LOOK!
O'HARA PROPERTY Hands off, O'Timminses!
PERFECT... PERFECT...
WE'LL MAKE A LITTLE BONFIRE...
IN THE NAME OF THE LAW, I'M ARRESTING YOU FOR DAMAGING PRIVATE PROPERTY!...
?!?
YOU SEEM TO BE FORGETTING, LUCKY LUKE, THAT I'M THE PAINFUL GULCH SHOOTING CHAMPION!...
WELL THEN, SHOOT THIS, CHAMP!...
BANG!
BANG!
BANG!
OK, OK, STOP WITH THE RAPID FIRE! I SURRENDER!
AND NOW, LET'S TURN THE SIGN AROUND!...
O'HARA PROPERTY Hands off, O'Timminses!
MORRIS & GOSCINNY
O'TIMMINS PROPERTY Hands off, O'Hara!

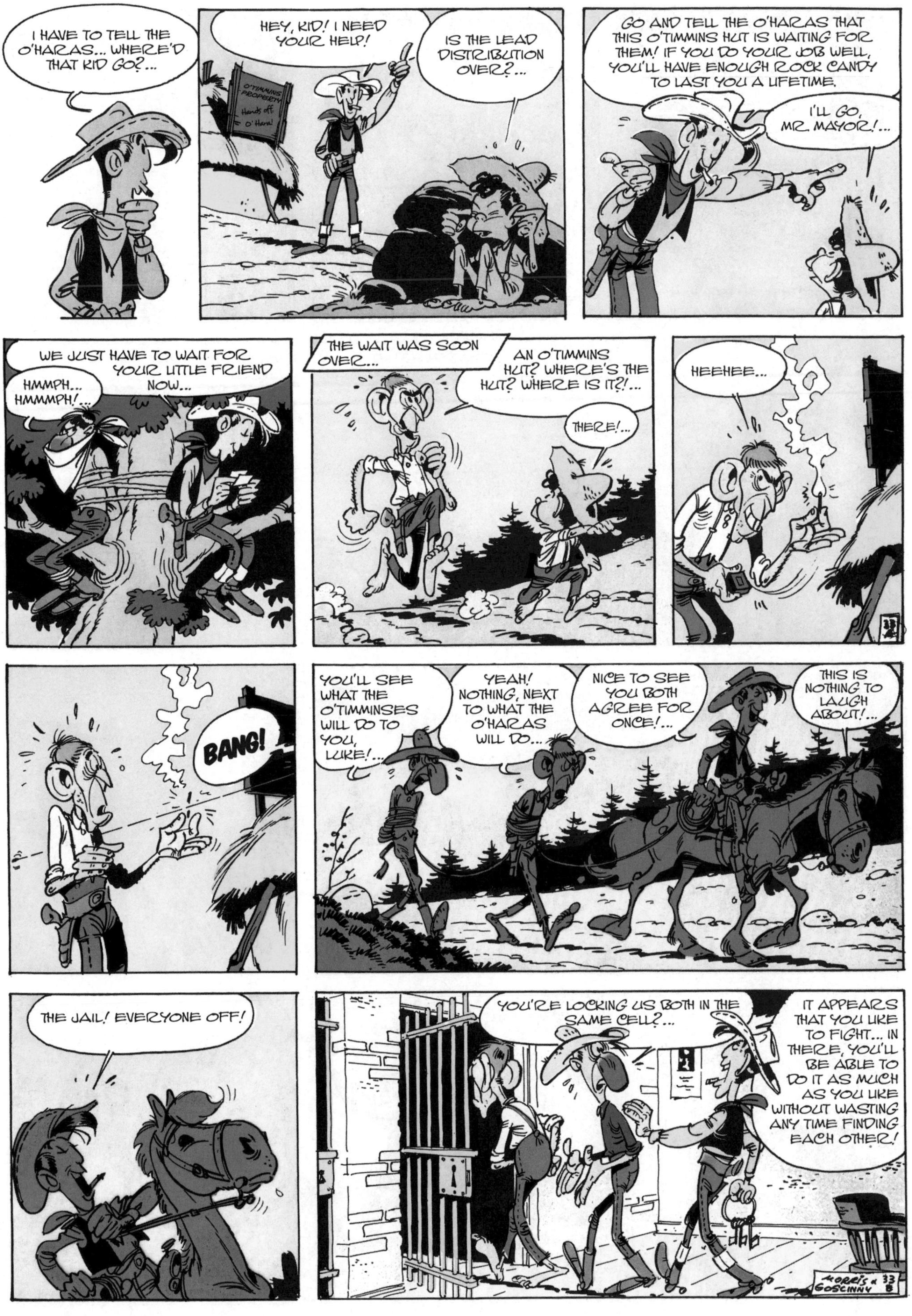
I HAVE TO TELL THE O'HARAS... WHERE'D THAT KID GO?...
HEY, KID! I NEED YOUR HELP!
IS THE LEAD DISTRIBUTION OVER?...
O'TIMMINS PROPERTY Hands off O'Hara!
GO AND TELL THE O'HARAS THAT THIS O'TIMMINS HUT IS WAITING FOR THEM! IF YOU DO YOUR JOB WELL, YOU'LL HAVE ENOUGH ROCK CANDY TO LAST YOU A LIFETIME.
I'LL GO, MR. MAYOR!...
WE JUST HAVE TO WAIT FOR YOUR LITTLE FRIEND NOW...
HMMPH... HMMMPH!...
THE WAIT WAS SOON OVER...
AN O'TIMMINS HUT? WHERE'S THE HUT? WHERE IS IT?!...
THERE!...
HEEHEE...
BANG!
YOU'LL SEE WHAT THE O'TIMMINSES WILL DO TO YOU, LUKE!...
YEAH! NOTHING, NEXT TO WHAT THE O'HARAS WILL DO...
NICE TO SEE YOU BOTH AGREE FOR ONCE!...
THIS IS NOTHING TO LAUGH ABOUT!...
THE JAIL! EVERYONE OFF!
YOU'RE LOCKING US BOTH IN THE SAME CELL?...
IT APPEARS THAT YOU LIKE TO FIGHT... IN THERE, YOU'LL BE ABLE TO DO IT AS MUCH AS YOU LIKE WITHOUT WASTING ANY TIME FINDING EACH OTHER!
MORRIS & GOSCINNY

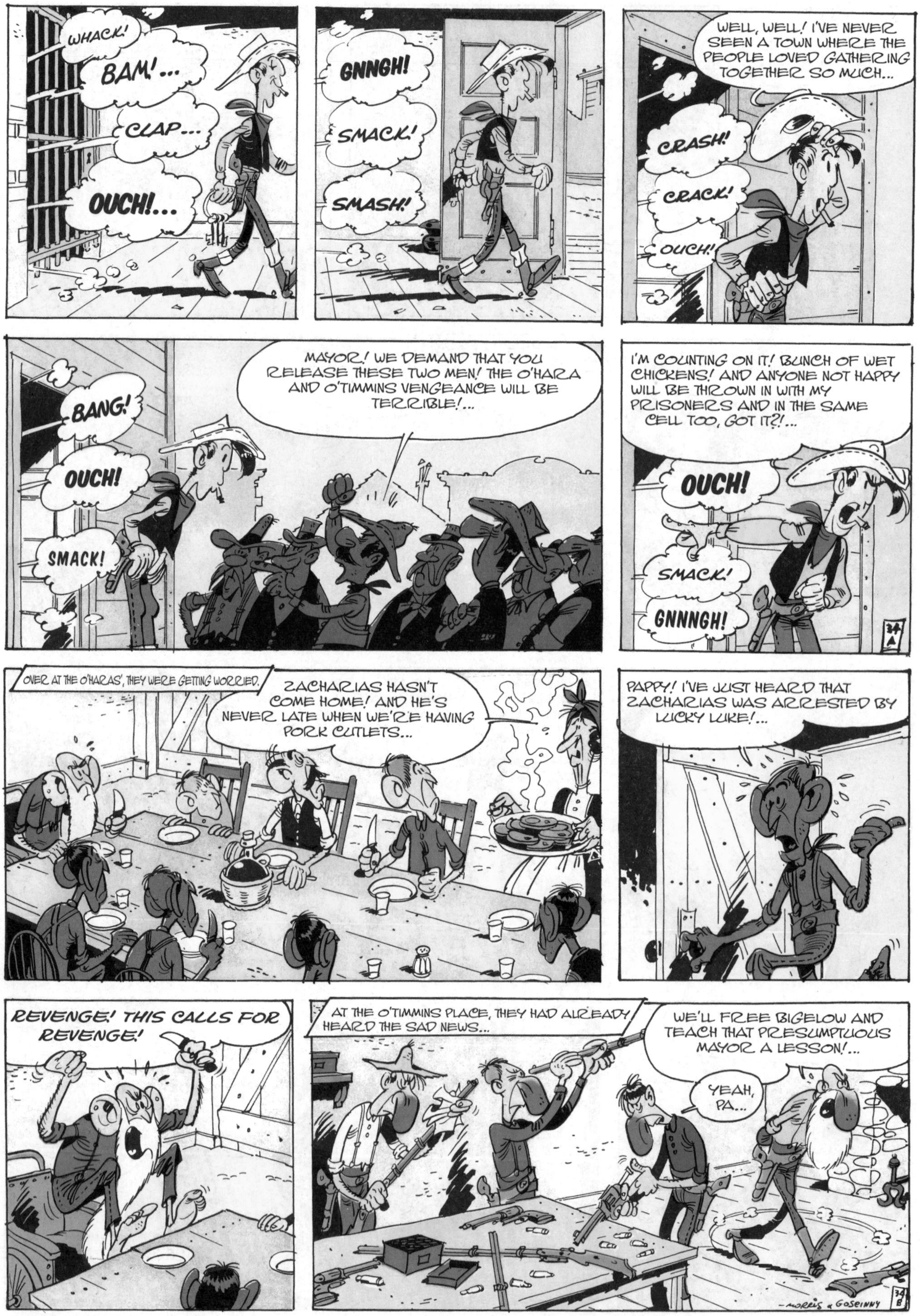

WHACK!
BAM!...
CLAP...
OUCH!...
GNNGH!
SMACK!
SMASH!
WELL, WELL! I'VE NEVER SEEN A TOWN WHERE THE PEOPLE LOVED GATHERING TOGETHER SO MUCH...
CRASH!
CRACK!
OUCH!
MAYOR! WE DEMAND THAT YOU RELEASE THESE TWO MEN! THE O'HARA AND O'TIMMINS VENGEANCE WILL BE TERRIBLE!...
BANG!
OUCH!
SMACK!
I'M COUNTING ON IT! BUNCH OF WET CHICKENS! AND ANYONE NOT HAPPY WILL BE THROWN IN WITH MY PRISONERS AND IN THE SAME CELL TOO, GOT IT?!...
OUCH!
SMACK!
GNNNGH!
OVER AT THE O'HARAS', THEY WERE GETTING WORRIED.
ZACHARIAS HASN'T COME HOME! AND HE'S NEVER LATE WHEN WE'RE HAVING PORK CUTLETS...
PAPPY! I'VE JUST HEARD THAT ZACHARIAS WAS ARRESTED BY LUCKY LUKE!...
REVENGE! THIS CALLS FOR REVENGE!
AT THE O'TIMMINS PLACE, THEY HAD ALREADY HEARD THE SAD NEWS...
WE'LL FREE BIGELOW AND TEACH THAT PRESUMPTUOUS MAYOR A LESSON!...
YEAH, PA...
MORRIS & GOSCINNY

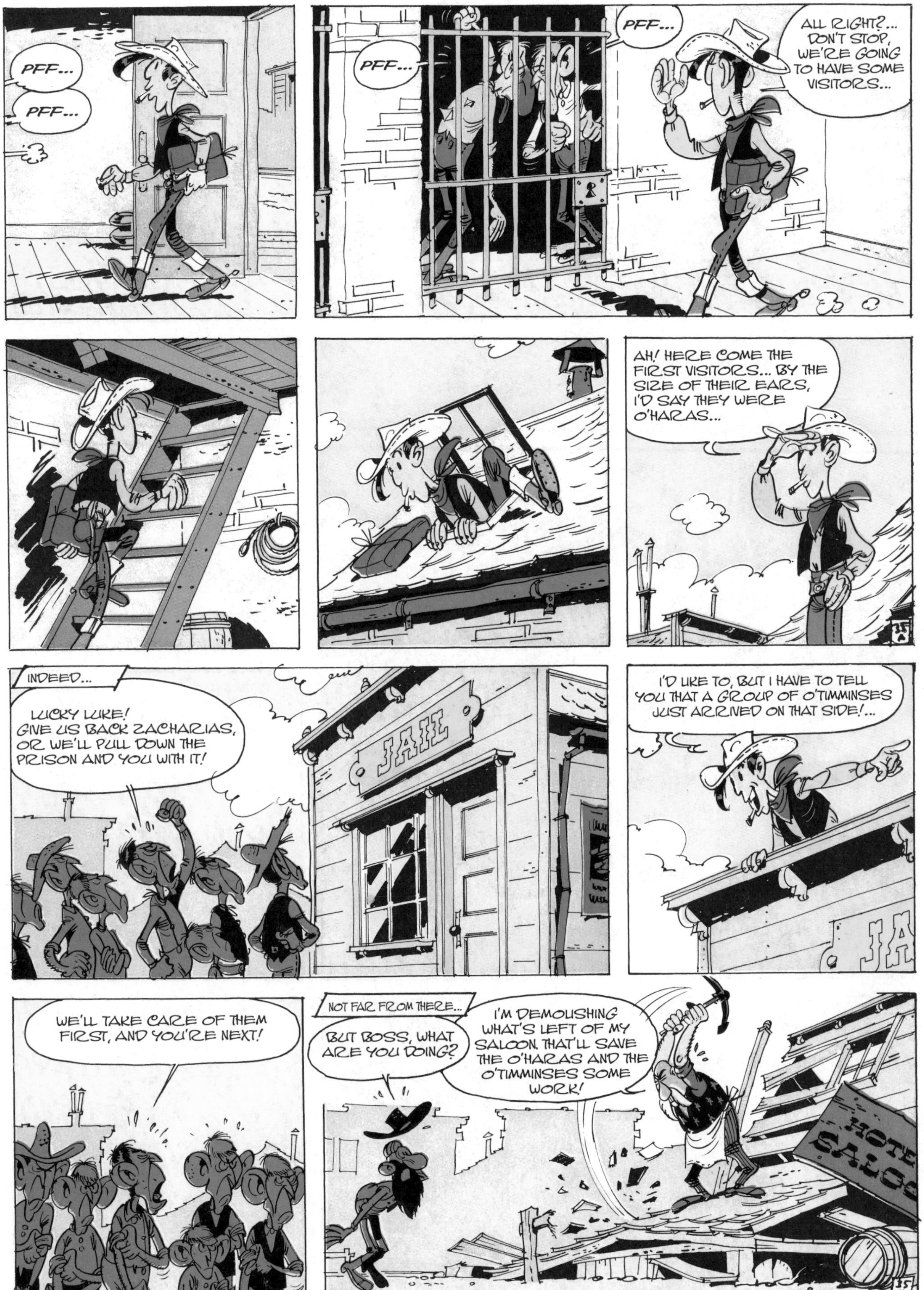
PFF...
PFF...
PFF...
PFF...
ALL RIGHT?... DON'T STOP, WE'RE GOING TO HAVE SOME VISITORS...
AH! HERE COME THE FIRST VISITORS... BY THE SIZE OF THEIR EARS, I'D SAY THEY WERE O'HARAS...
INDEED...
LUCKY LUKE! GIVE US BACK ZACHARIAS, OR WE'LL PULL DOWN THE PRISON AND YOU WITH IT!
JAIL
I'D LIKE TO, BUT I HAVE TO TELL YOU THAT A GROUP OF O'TIMMINSES JUST ARRIVED ON THAT SIDE!...
WE'LL TAKE CARE OF THEM FIRST, AND YOU'RE NEXT!
NOT FAR FROM THERE...
BUT BOSS, WHAT ARE YOU DOING?
I'M DEMOLISHING WHAT'S LEFT OF MY SALOON. THAT'LL SAVE THE O'HARAS AND THE O'TIMMINSES SOME WORK!
MORRIS et GOSCINNY

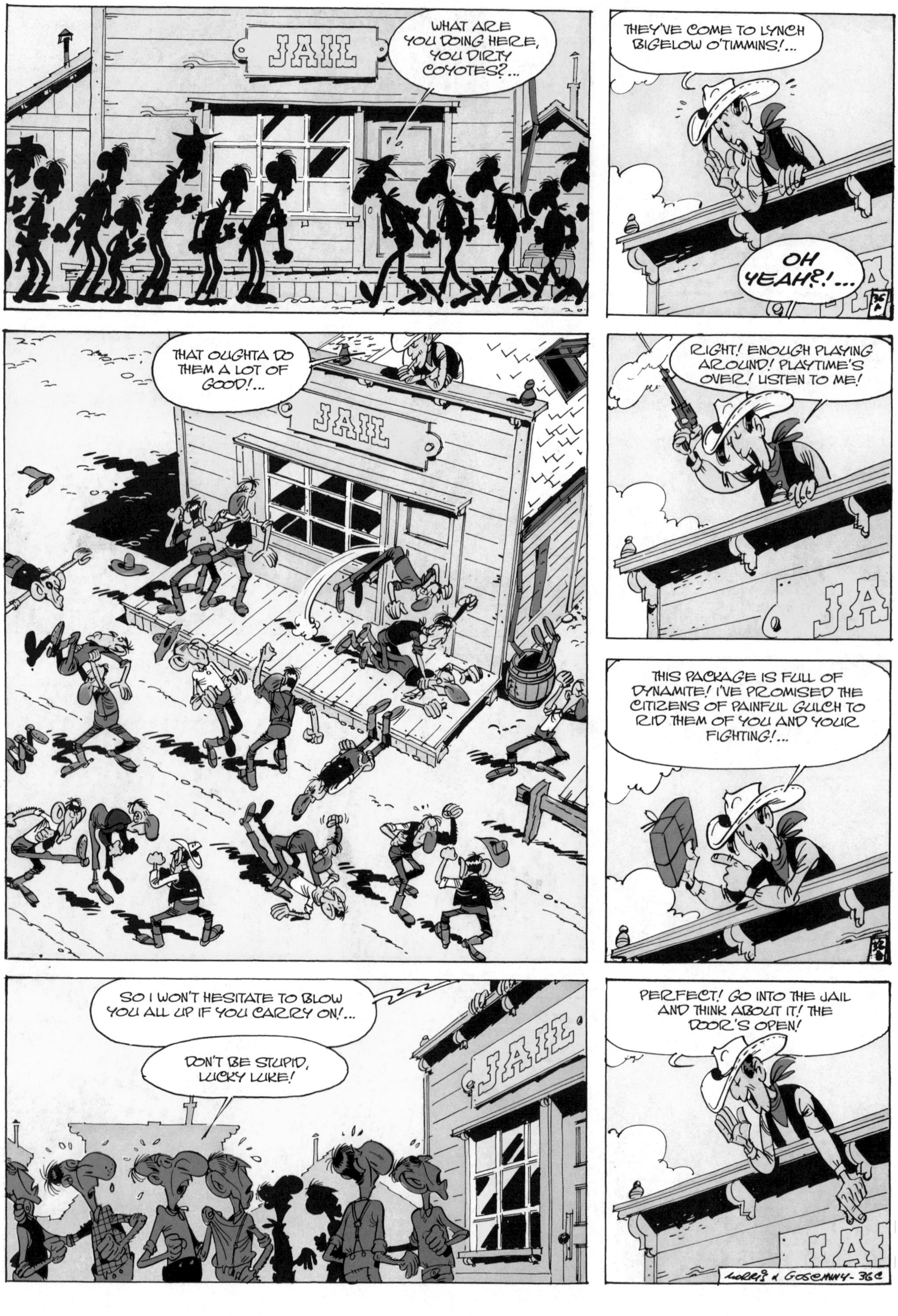

JAIL
WHAT ARE YOU DOING HERE, YOU DIRTY COYOTES?...
THEY'VE COME TO LYNCH BIGELOW O'TIMMINS!...
OH YEAH?!...
THAT OUGHTA DO THEM A LOT OF GOOD!...
JAIL
RIGHT! ENOUGH PLAYING AROUND! PLAYTIME'S OVER! LISTEN TO ME!
THIS PACKAGE IS FULL OF DYNAMITE! I'VE PROMISED THE CITIZENS OF PAINFUL GULCH TO RID THEM OF YOU AND YOUR FIGHTING!...
SO I WON'T HESITATE TO BLOW YOU ALL UP IF YOU CARRY ON!...
DON'T BE STUPID, LUCKY LUKE!
JAIL
PERFECT! GO INTO THE JAIL AND THINK ABOUT IT! THE DOOR'S OPEN!

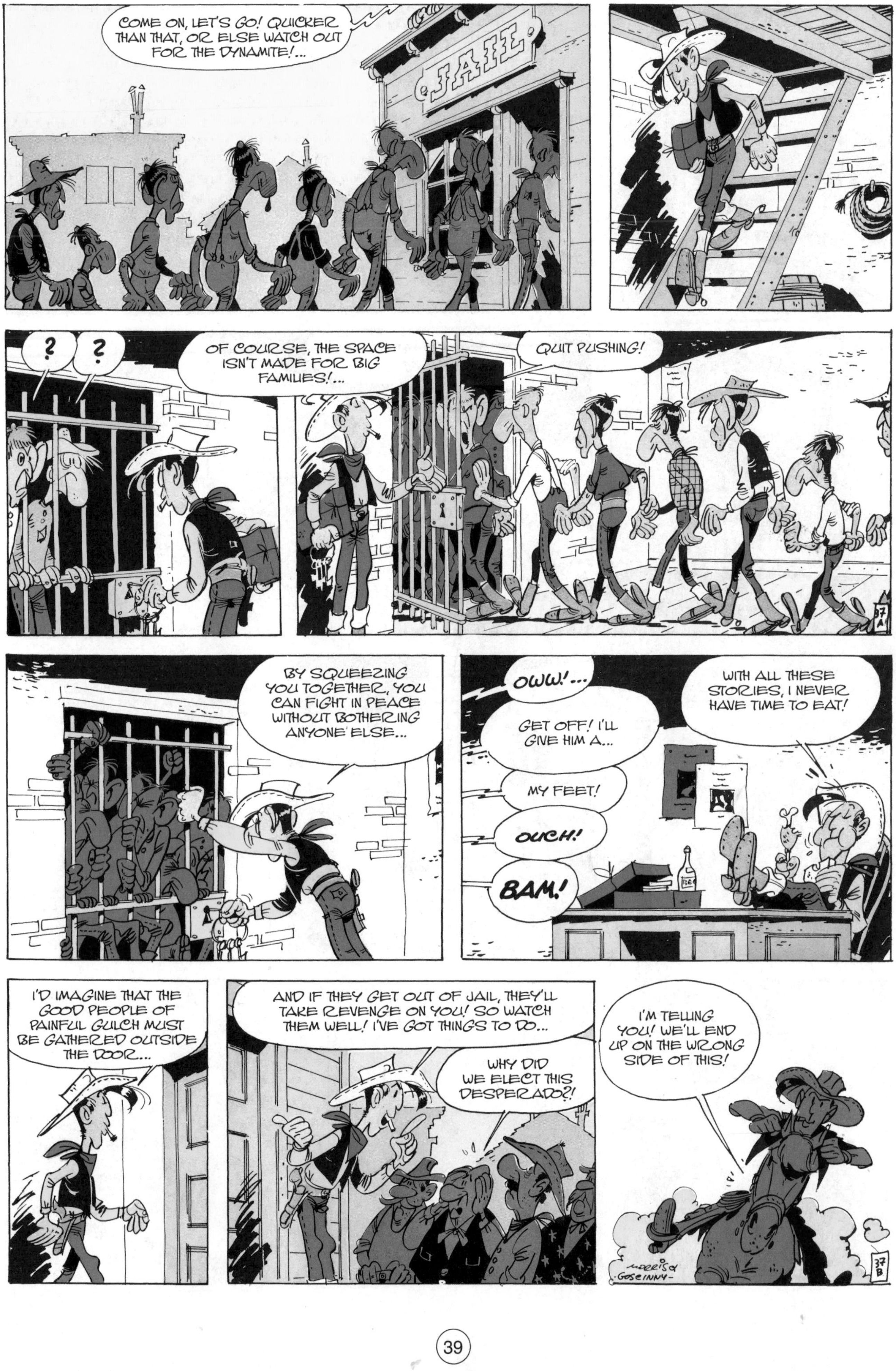
COME ON, LET'S GO! QUICKER THAN THAT, OR ELSE WATCH OUT FOR THE DYNAMITE!...
JAIL
?
?
OF COURSE, THE SPACE ISN'T MADE FOR BIG FAMILIES!...
QUIT PUSHING!
BY SQUEEZING YOU TOGETHER, YOU CAN FIGHT IN PEACE WITHOUT BOTHERING ANYONE ELSE...
OWW!...
GET OFF! I'LL GIVE HIM A...
MY FEET!
OUCH!
BAM!
WITH ALL THESE STORIES, I NEVER HAVE TIME TO EAT!
I'D IMAGINE THAT THE GOOD PEOPLE OF PAINFUL GULCH MUST BE GATHERED OUTSIDE THE DOOR...
AND IF THEY GET OUT OF JAIL, THEY'LL TAKE REVENGE ON YOU! SO WATCH THEM WELL! I'VE GOT THINGS TO DO...
WHY DID WE ELECT THIS DESPERADO?!
I'M TELLING YOU! WE'LL END UP ON THE WRONG SIDE OF THIS!
MORRIS
GOSCINNY

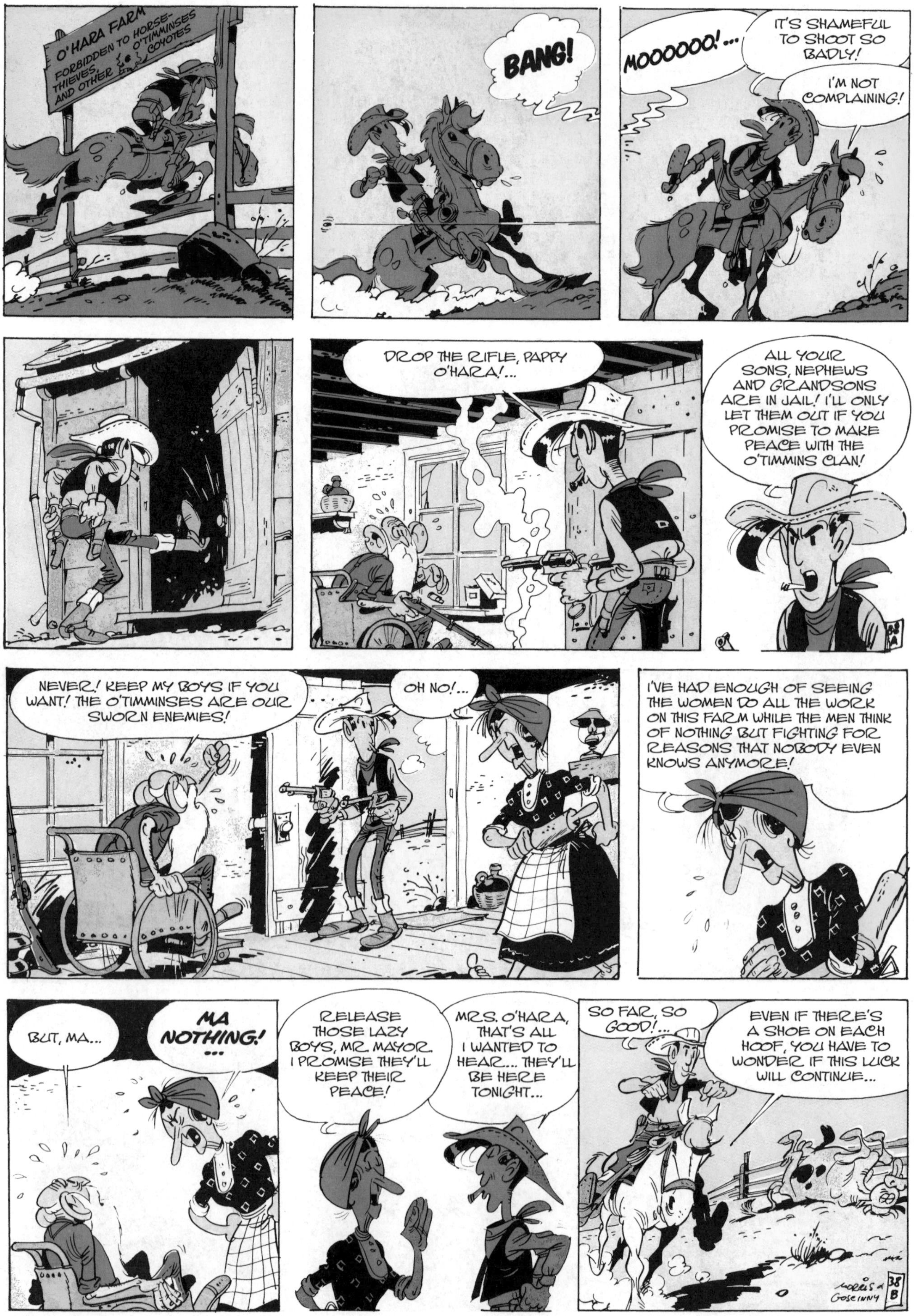
O'HARA FARM
FORBIDDEN TO HORSE-THIEVES, O'TIMMINSES AND OTHER COYOTES
BANG!
MOOOOOO!...
IT'S SHAMEFUL TO SHOOT SO BADLY!
I'M NOT COMPLAINING!
DROP THE RIFLE, PAPPY O'HARA!...
ALL YOUR SONS, NEPHEWS AND GRANDSONS ARE IN JAIL! I'LL ONLY LET THEM OUT IF YOU PROMISE TO MAKE PEACE WITH THE O'TIMMINS CLAN!
NEVER! KEEP MY BOYS IF YOU WANT! THE O'TIMMINSES ARE OUR SWORN ENEMIES!
OH NO!...
I'VE HAD ENOUGH OF SEEING THE WOMEN DO ALL THE WORK ON THIS FARM WHILE THE MEN THINK OF NOTHING BUT FIGHTING FOR REASONS THAT NOBODY EVEN KNOWS ANYMORE!
BUT, MA...
MA NOTHING!...
RELEASE THOSE LAZY BOYS, MR. MAYOR. I PROMISE THEY'LL KEEP THEIR PEACE!
MRS. O'HARA, THAT'S ALL I WANTED TO HEAR... THEY'LL BE HERE TONIGHT...
SO FAR, SO GOOD!...
EVEN IF THERE'S A SHOE ON EACH HOOF, YOU HAVE TO WONDER IF THIS LUCK WILL CONTINUE...
MORRIS & GOSCINNY

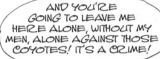

O'TIMMINS FARM
WE HAVE WHAT WE NEED TO DEFEND OURSELVES AGAINST RATTLESNAKES, PESTS AND O'HARAS

I'LL GIVE YOU TWO SECONDS TO SCRAM!

I'VE JUST COME TO TELL YOU THAT I'LL RELEASE THE O'HARAS...

AND YOU'RE GOING TO LEAVE ME HERE ALONE, WITHOUT MY MEN, ALONE AGAINST THOSE COYOTES! IT'S A CRIME!

IF YOU PROMISE TO MAKE PEACE WITH THE O'HARAS, I'LL SET YOUR MEN FREE!...

NEVER! YOU HEAR ME, MAYOR? NEVER!

I HEAR YOU! THEN I'LL JUST HAVE TO LEAVE THEN...

MRS. O'HARA WAS MORE REASONABLE THAN YOU...

MRS. O'HARA IS RIGHT! I'VE HAD ENOUGH OF THESE ROUGHNECKS AND THEIR STUPID RIVALRY!...

LET MY ROUGHNECKS GO, MR. MAYOR, AND I PROMISE YOU THAT THEY WON'T TOUCH THE O'HARA ROUGHNECKS!...

BUT, DARLING...

BUT WHAT?...

CALM DOWN, DARLING... CALM DOWN...

ROUGH-NECK!...

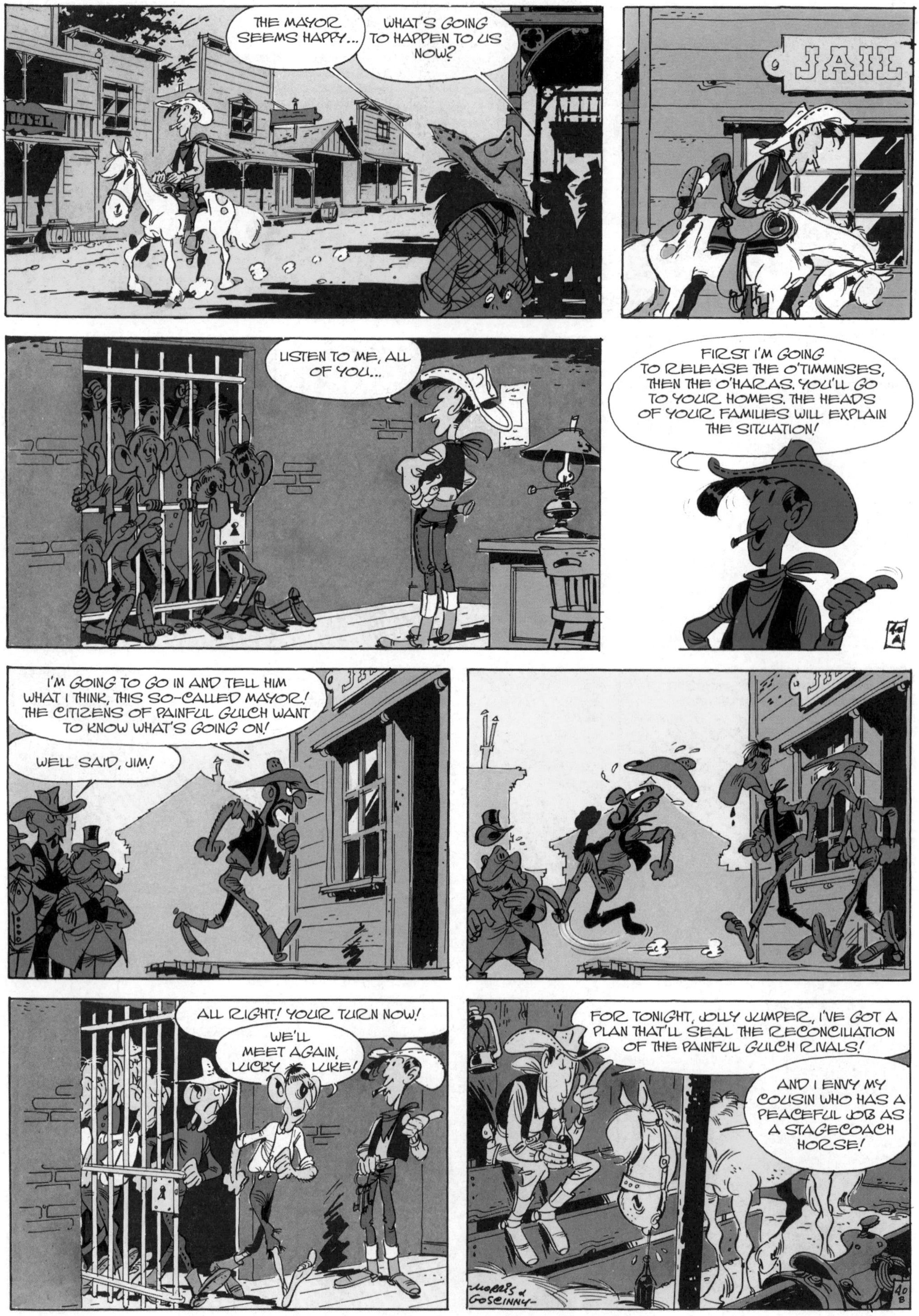
THE MAYOR SEEMS HAPPY...
WHAT'S GOING TO HAPPEN TO US NOW?
JAIL
LISTEN TO ME, ALL OF YOU...
FIRST I'M GOING TO RELEASE THE O'TIMMINSES, THEN THE O'HARAS. YOU'LL GO TO YOUR HOMES. THE HEADS OF YOUR FAMILIES WILL EXPLAIN THE SITUATION!
I'M GOING TO GO IN AND TELL HIM WHAT I THINK, THIS SO-CALLED MAYOR! THE CITIZENS OF PAINFUL GULCH WANT TO KNOW WHAT'S GOING ON!
WELL SAID, JIM!
ALL RIGHT! YOUR TURN NOW!
WE'LL MEET AGAIN, LUCKY LUKE!
FOR TONIGHT, JOLLY JUMPER, I'VE GOT A PLAN THAT'LL SEAL THE RECONCILIATION OF THE PAINFUL GULCH RIVALS!
AND I ENVY MY COUSIN WHO HAS A PEACEFUL JOB AS A STAGECOACH HORSE!
MORRIS & GOSCINNY

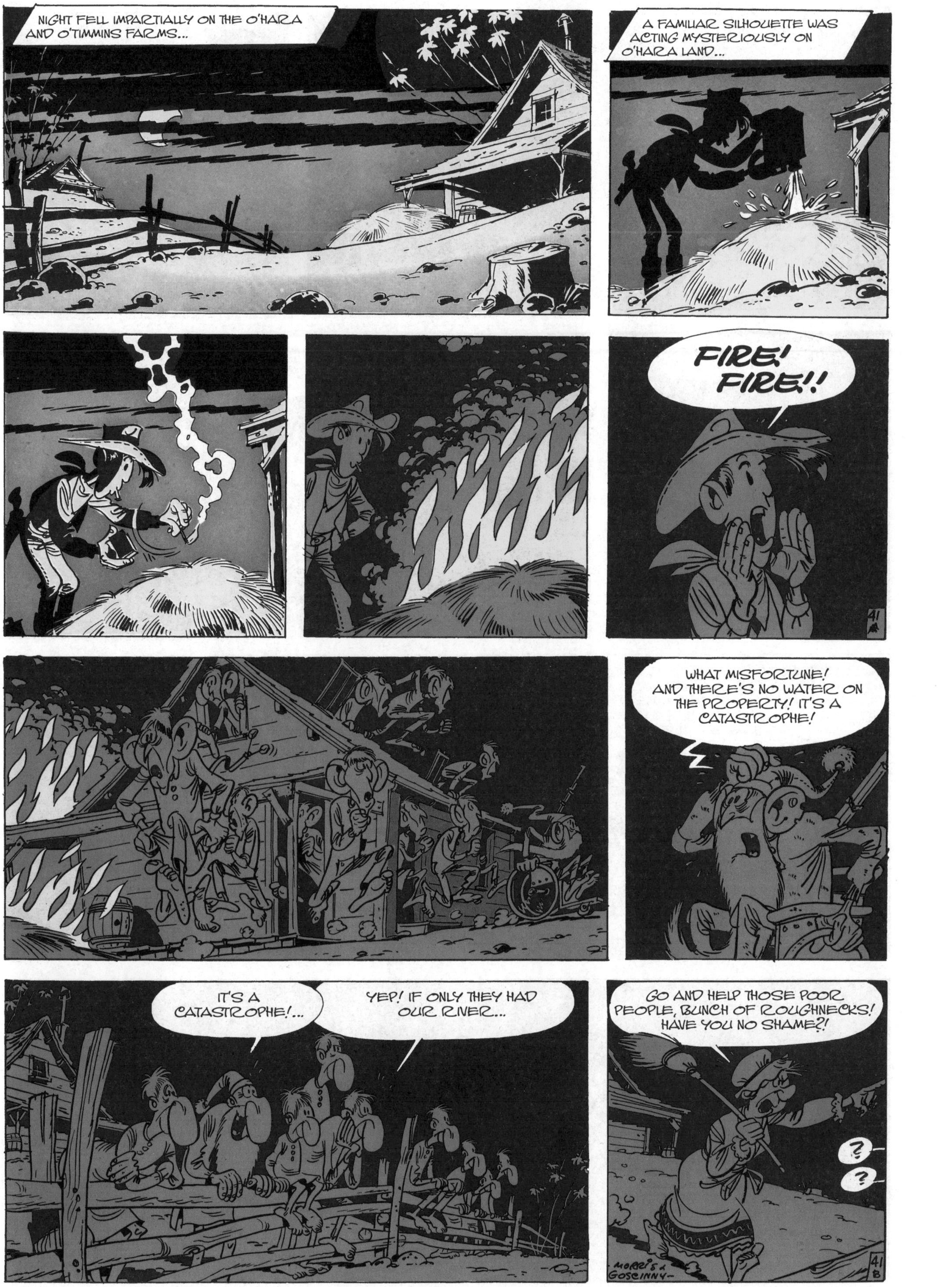
NIGHT FELL IMPARTIALLY ON THE O'HARA AND O'TIMMINS FARMS...
A FAMILIAR SILHOUETTE WAS ACTING MYSTERIOUSLY ON O'HARA LAND...
FIRE! FIRE!!
WHAT MISFORTUNE! AND THERE'S NO WATER ON THE PROPERTY! IT'S A CATASTROPHE!
IT'S A CATASTROPHE!...
YEP! IF ONLY THEY HAD OUR RIVER...
GO AND HELP THOSE POOR PEOPLE, BUNCH OF ROUGHNECKS! HAVE YOU NO SHAME?!
?
?
MORRIS & GOSCINNY

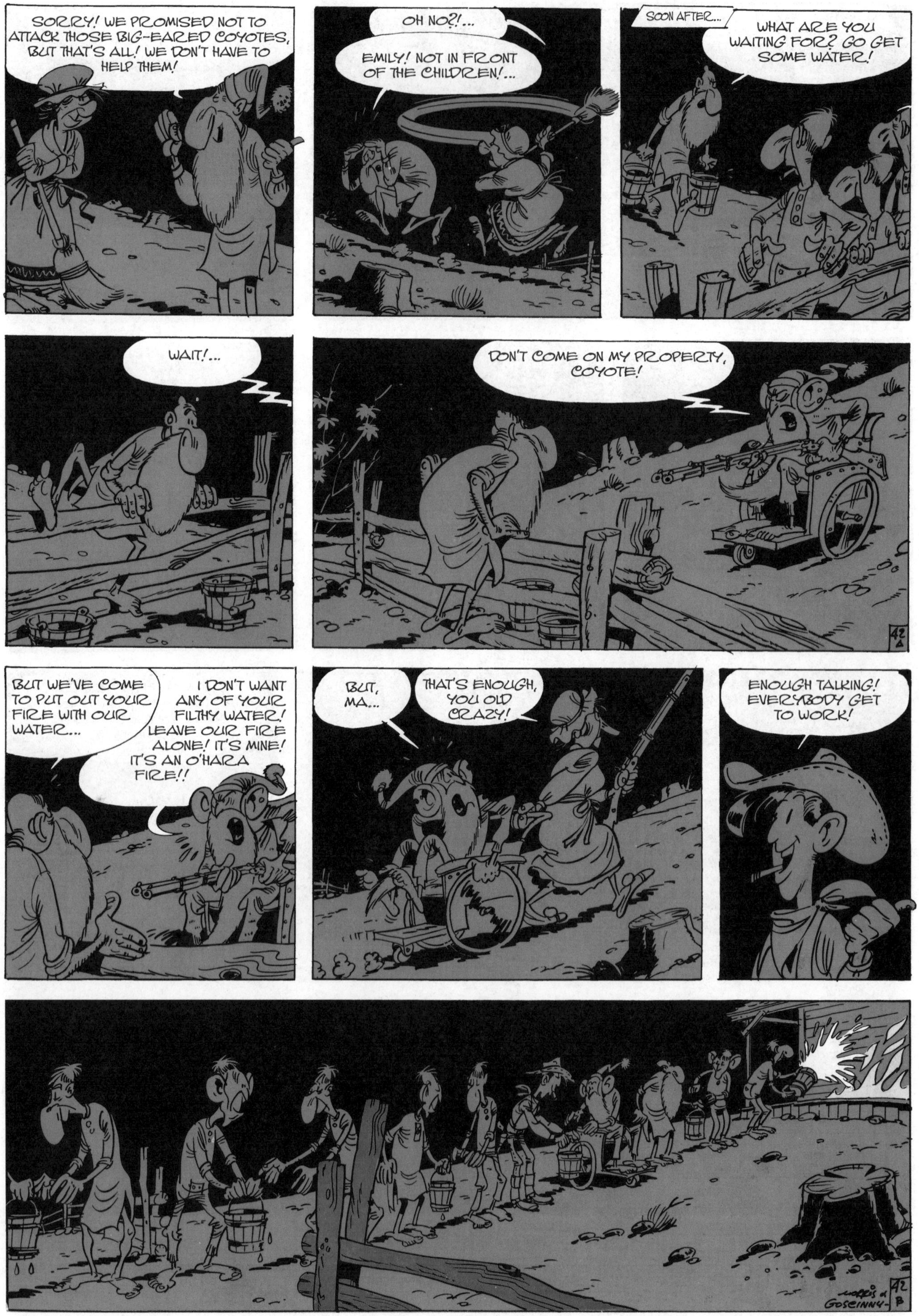
SORRY! WE PROMISED NOT TO ATTACK THOSE BIG-EARED COYOTES, BUT THAT'S ALL! WE DON'T HAVE TO HELP THEM!
OH NO?!...
EMILY! NOT IN FRONT OF THE CHILDREN!...
SOON AFTER...
WHAT ARE YOU WAITING FOR? GO GET SOME WATER!
WAIT!...
DON'T COME ON MY PROPERTY, COYOTE!
BUT WE'VE COME TO PUT OUT YOUR FIRE WITH OUR WATER...
I DON'T WANT ANY OF YOUR FILTHY WATER! LEAVE OUR FIRE ALONE! IT'S MINE! IT'S AN O'HARA FIRE!!
BUT, MA...
THAT'S ENOUGH, YOU OLD CRAZY!
ENOUGH TALKING! EVERYBODY GET TO WORK!

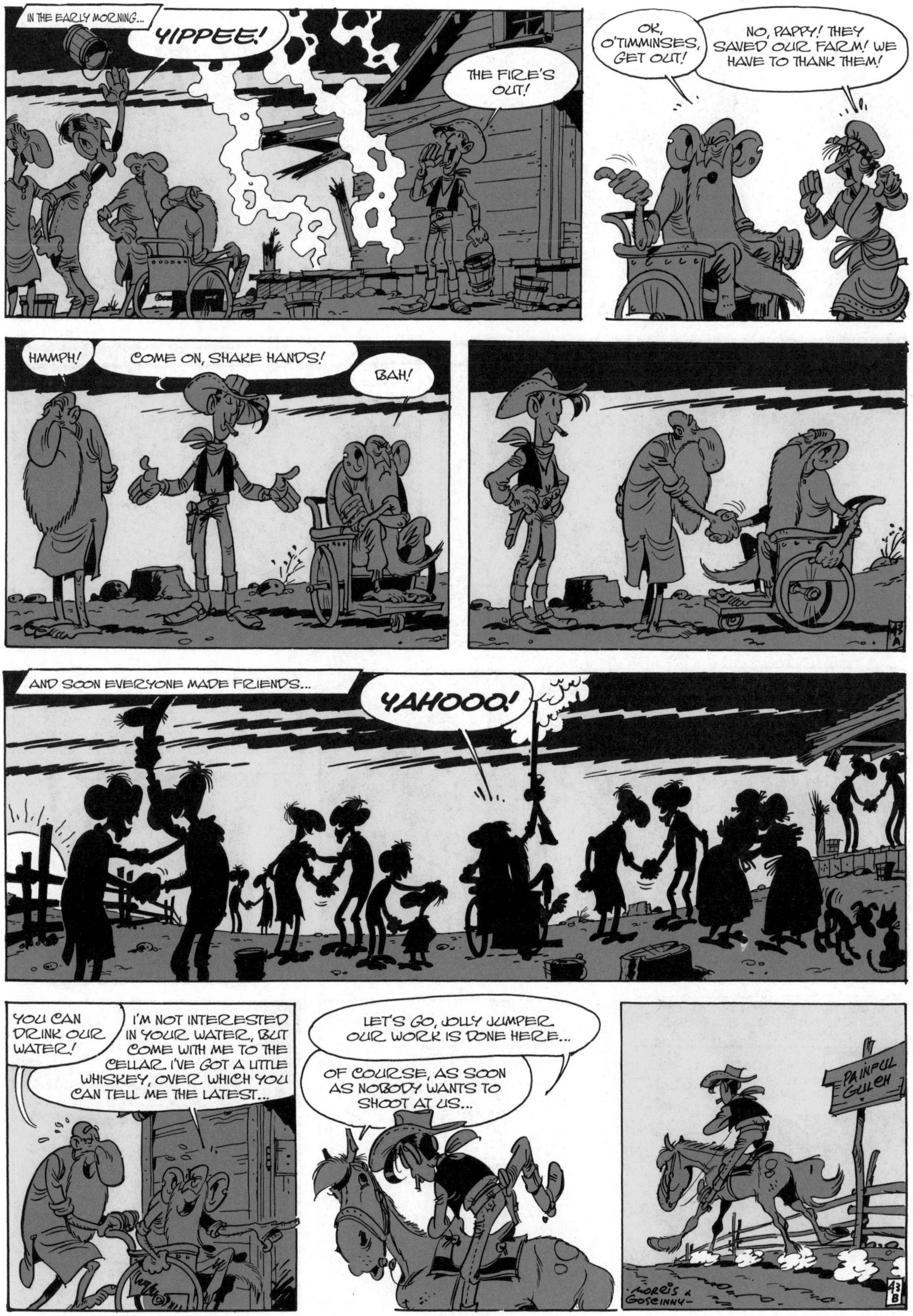
IN THE EARLY MORNING...
YIPPEE!
THE FIRE'S OUT!
OK, O'TIMMINSES, GET OUT!
NO, PAPPY! THEY SAVED OUR FARM! WE HAVE TO THANK THEM!
HMMPH!
COME ON, SHAKE HANDS!
BAH!
AND SOON EVERYONE MADE FRIENDS...
YAHOOO!
YOU CAN DRINK OUR WATER!
I'M NOT INTERESTED IN YOUR WATER, BUT COME WITH ME TO THE CELLAR. I'VE GOT A LITTLE WHISKEY, OVER WHICH YOU CAN TELL ME THE LATEST...
LET'S GO, JOLLY JUMPER OUR WORK IS DONE HERE...
OF COURSE, AS SOON AS NOBODY WANTS TO SHOOT AT US...
PAINFUL GULCH
MORRIS & GOSCINNY

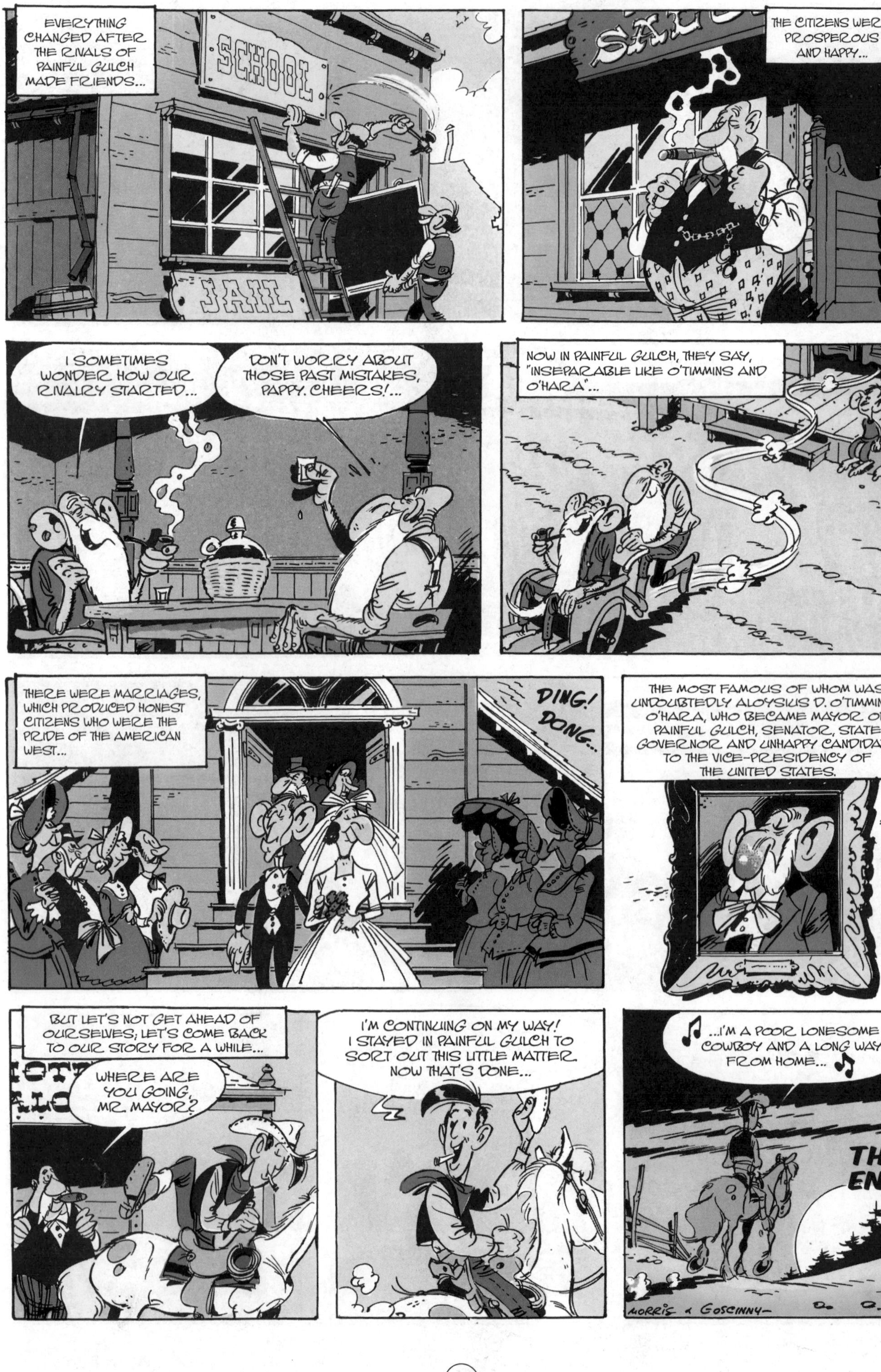
EVERYTHING CHANGED AFTER THE RIVALS OF PAINFUL GULCH MADE FRIENDS...
SCHOOL
JAIL
THE CITIZENS WERE PROSPEROUS AND HAPPY...
I SOMETIMES WONDER HOW OUR RIVALRY STARTED...
DON'T WORRY ABOUT THOSE PAST MISTAKES, PAPPY. CHEERS!...
NOW IN PAINFUL GULCH, THEY SAY, "INSEPARABLE LIKE O'TIMMINS AND O'HARA"...
THERE WERE MARRIAGES, WHICH PRODUCED HONEST CITIZENS WHO WERE THE PRIDE OF THE AMERICAN WEST...
DING! DONG...
THE MOST FAMOUS OF WHOM WAS UNDOUBTEDLY ALOYSIUS D. O'TIMMINS-O'HARA, WHO BECAME MAYOR OF PAINFUL GULCH, SENATOR, STATE GOVERNOR AND UNHAPPY CANDIDATE TO THE VICE-PRESIDENCY OF THE UNITED STATES.
BUT LET'S NOT GET AHEAD OF OURSELVES; LET'S COME BACK TO OUR STORY FOR A WHILE...
WHERE ARE YOU GOING, MR. MAYOR?
I'M CONTINUING ON MY WAY! I STAYED IN PAINFUL GULCH TO SORT OUT THIS LITTLE MATTER. NOW THAT'S DONE...
...I'M A POOR LONESOME COWBOY AND A LONG WAY FROM HOME...
THE END
MORRIS & GOSCINNY

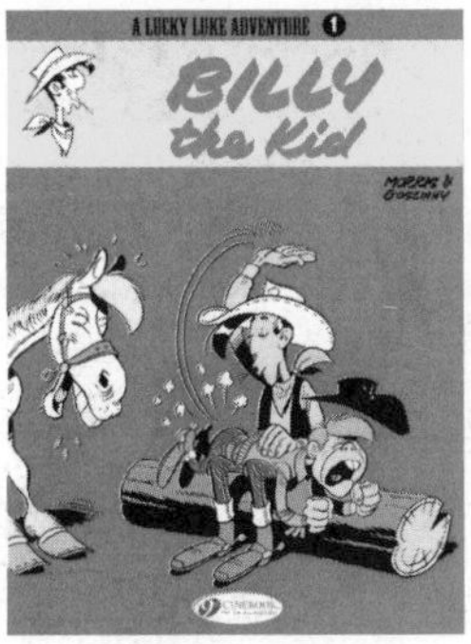
A LUCKY LUKE ADVENTURE 1
BILLY the Kid

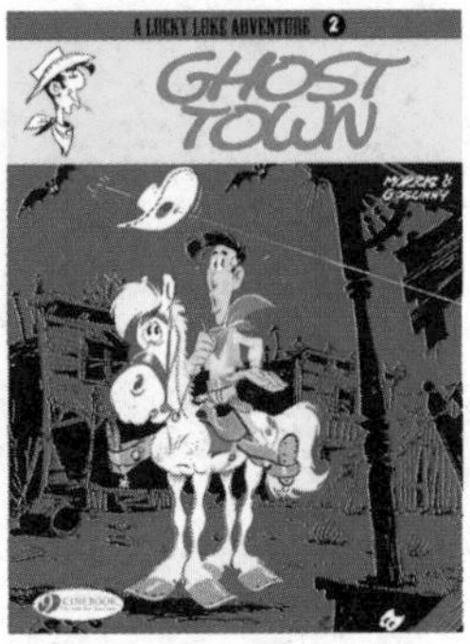
A LUCKY LUKE ADVENTURE 2
GHOST TOWN

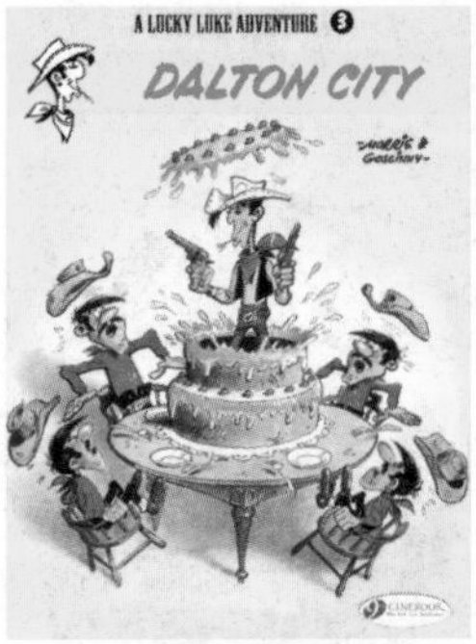
A LUCKY LUKE ADVENTURE 3
DALTON CITY

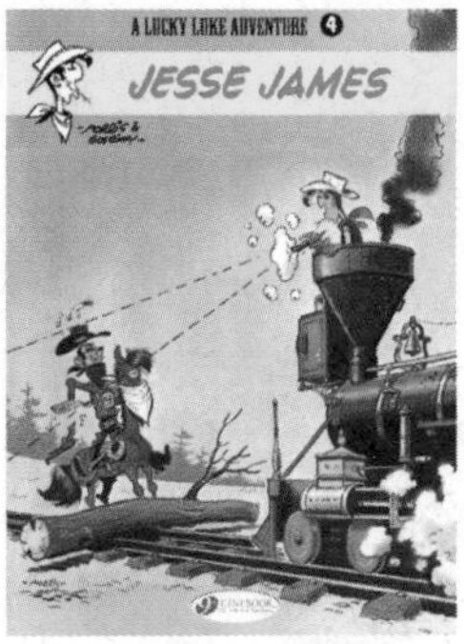
A LUCKY LUKE ADVENTURE 4
JESSE JAMES

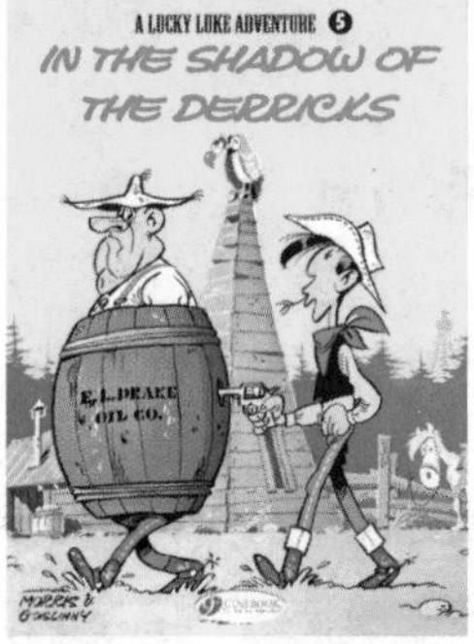
A LUCKY LUKE ADVENTURE 5
IN THE SHADOW OF THE DERRICKS

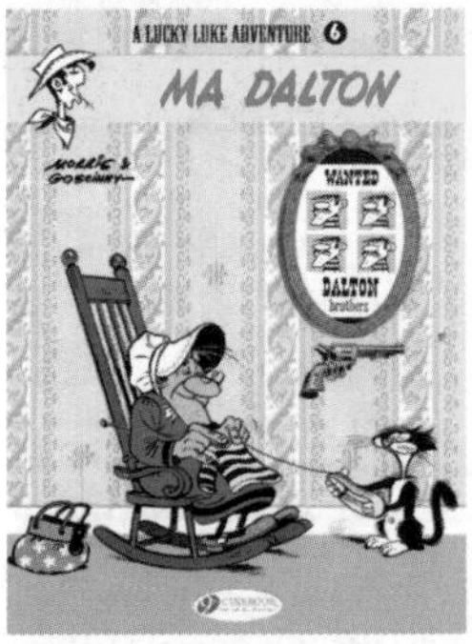
A LUCKY LUKE ADVENTURE 6
MA DALTON

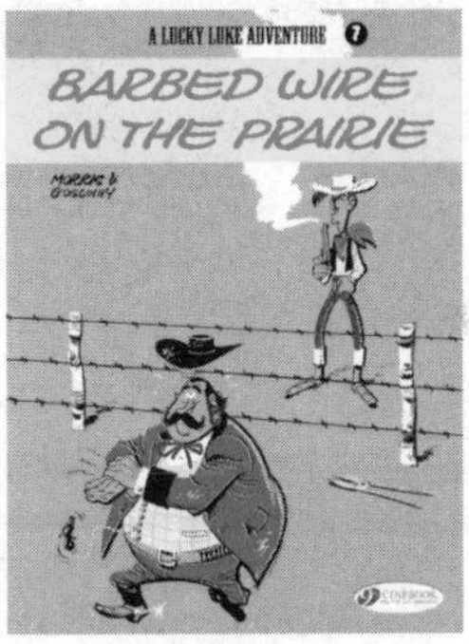
A LUCKY LUKE ADVENTURE 7
BARBED WIRE ON THE PRAIRIE

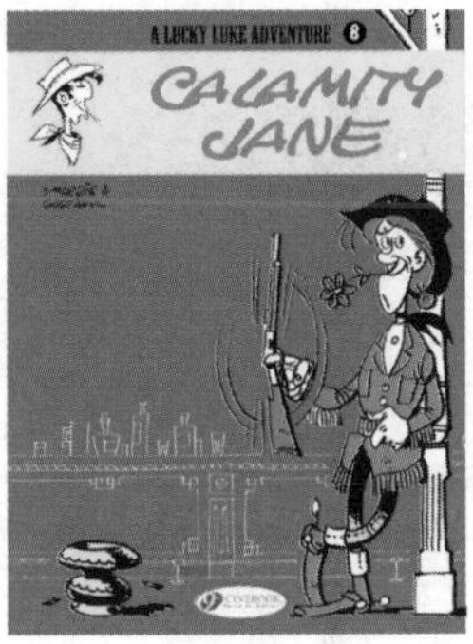
A LUCKY LUKE ADVENTURE 8
CALAMITY JANE

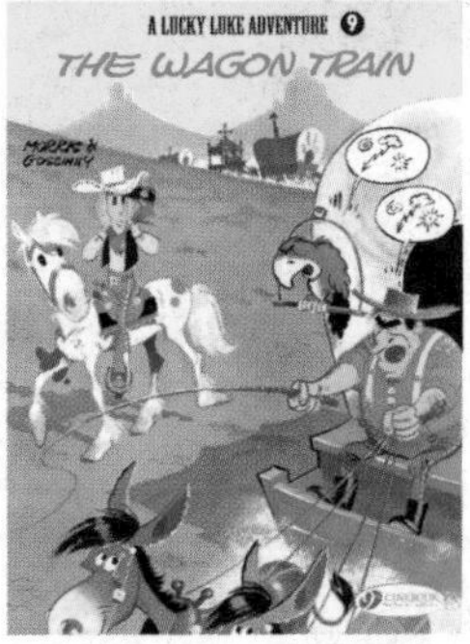
A LUCKY LUKE ADVENTURE 9
THE WAGON TRAIN

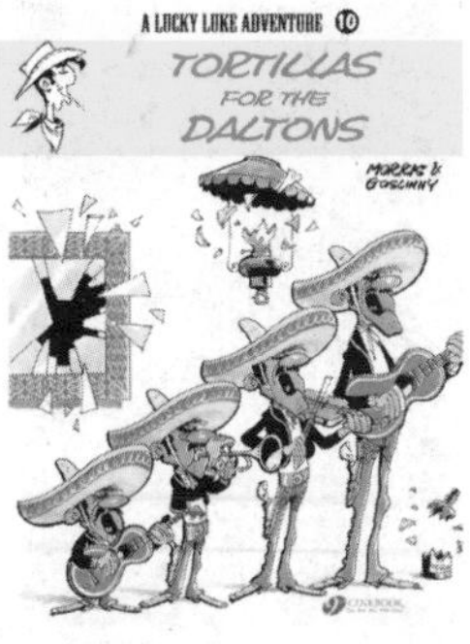
A LUCKY LUKE ADVENTURE 10
TORTILLAS FOR THE DALTONS

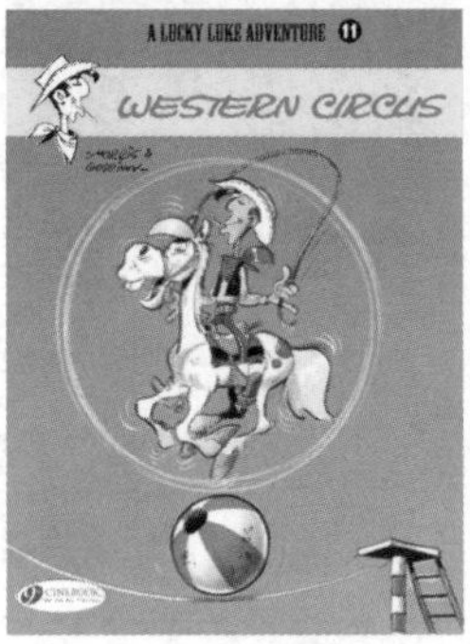
A LUCKY LUKE ADVENTURE 11
WESTERN CIRCUS

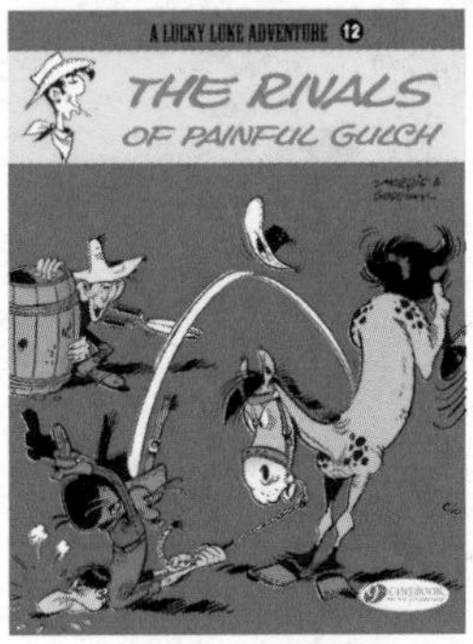
A LUCKY LUKE ADVENTURE 12
THE RIVALS OF PAINFUL GULCH

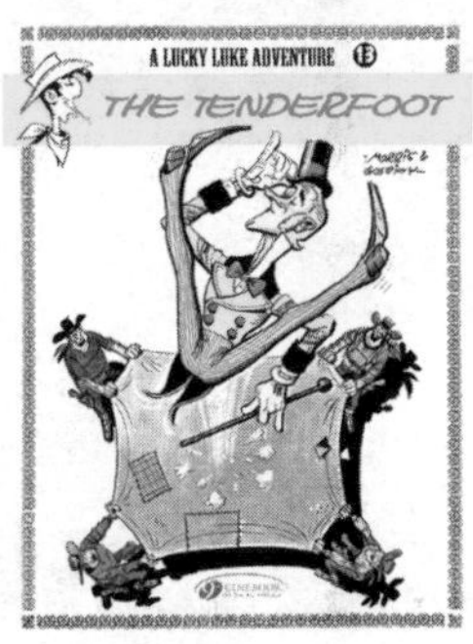
A LUCKY LUKE ADVENTURE 13
THE TENDERFOOT

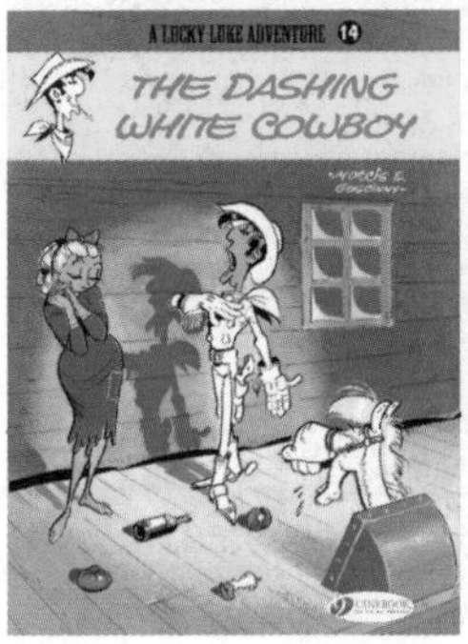
A LUCKY LUKE ADVENTURE 14
THE DASHING WHITE COWBOY

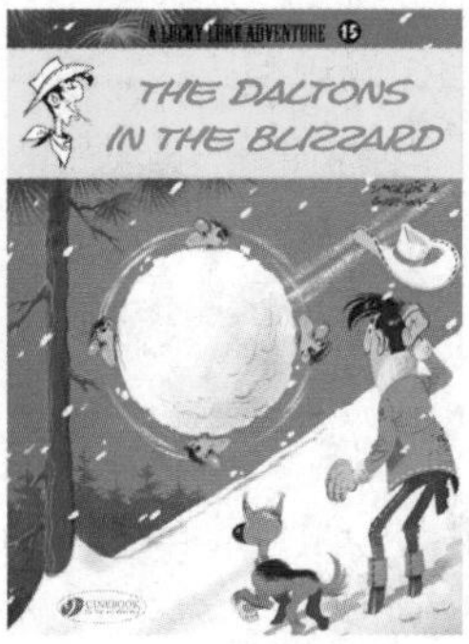
A LUCKY LUKE ADVENTURE 15
THE DALTONS IN THE BLIZZARD

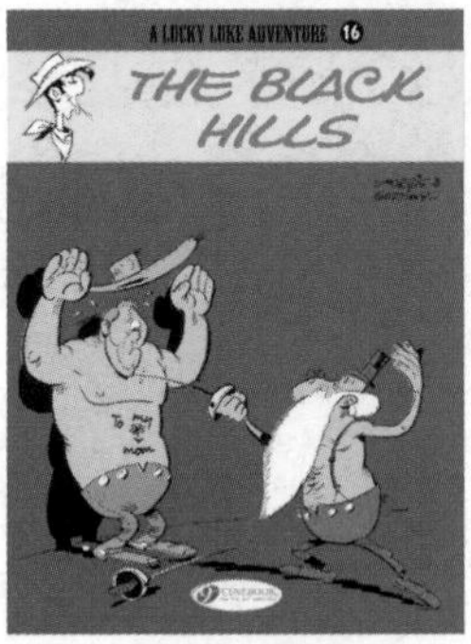
A LUCKY LUKE ADVENTURE 16
THE BLACK HILLS

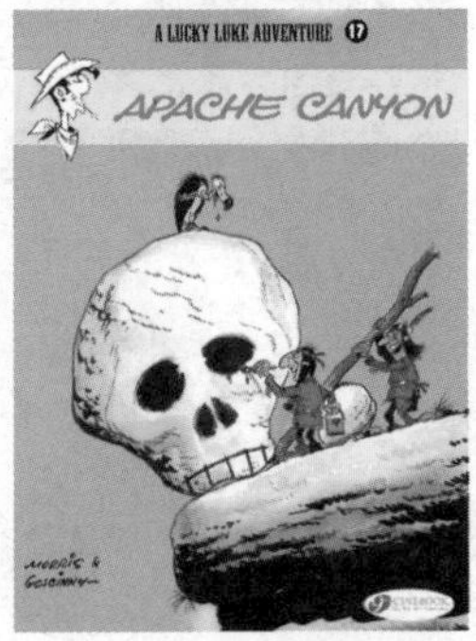
A LUCKY LUKE ADVENTURE 17
APACHE CANYON

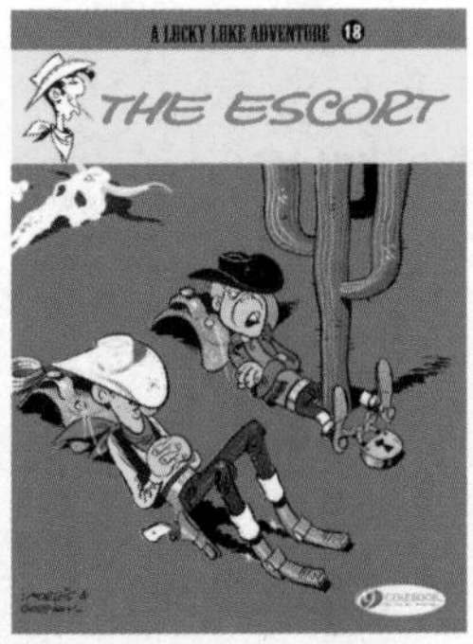
A LUCKY LUKE ADVENTURE 18
THE ESCORT

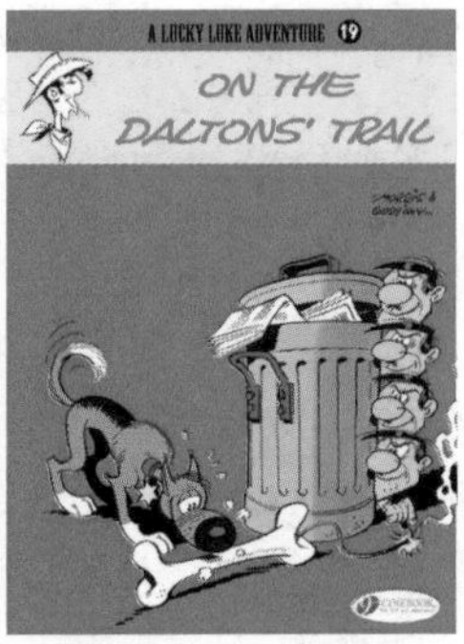
A LUCKY LUKE ADVENTURE 19
ON THE DALTONS' TRAIL

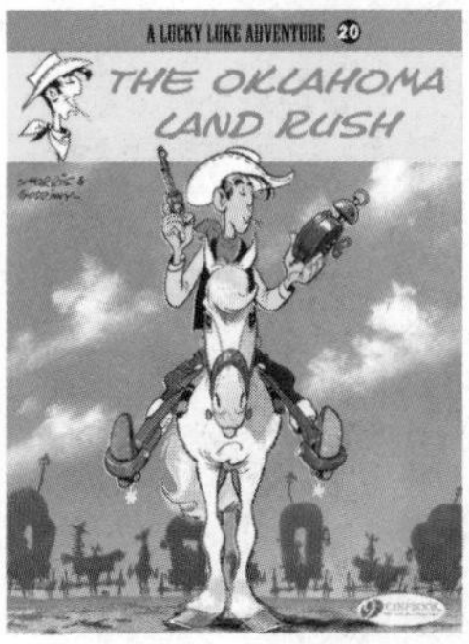
A LUCKY LUKE ADVENTURE 20
THE OKLAHOMA LAND RUSH

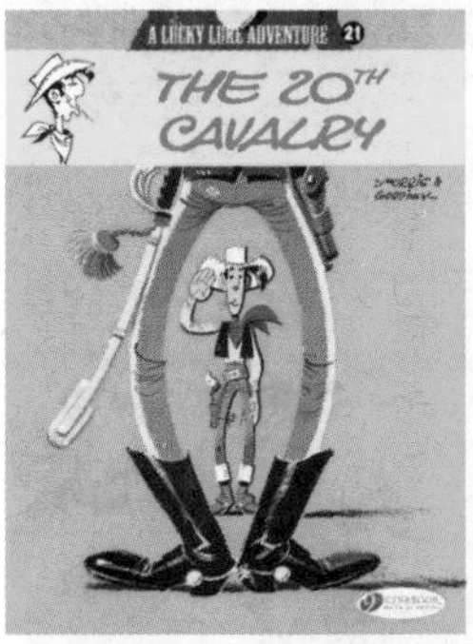
A LUCKY LUKE ADVENTURE 21
THE 20TH CAVALRY

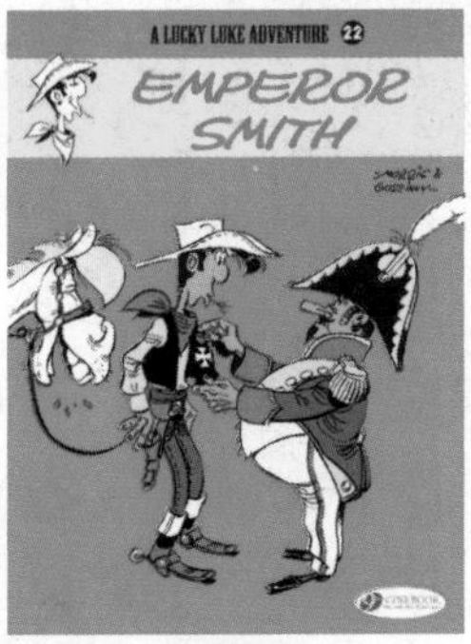
A LUCKY LUKE ADVENTURE 22
EMPEROR SMITH

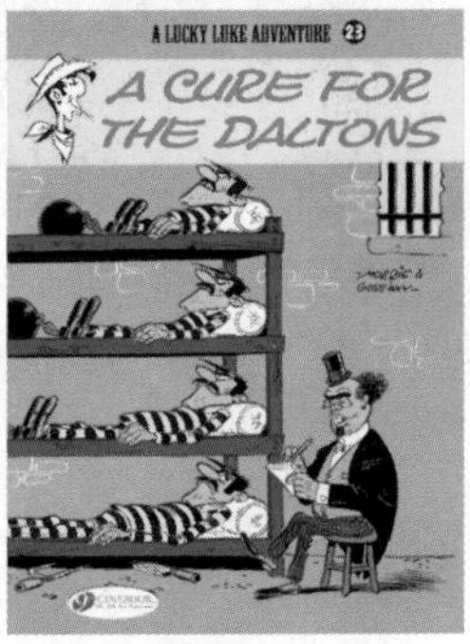
A LUCKY LUKE ADVENTURE 23
A CURE FOR THE DALTONS

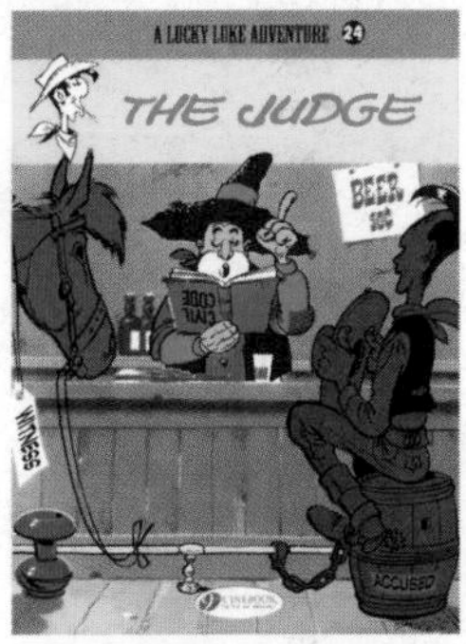
A LUCKY LUKE ADVENTURE 24
THE JUDGE

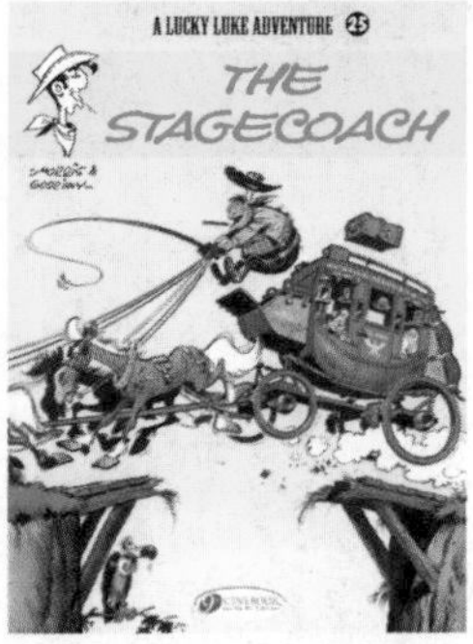
A LUCKY LUKE ADVENTURE 25
THE STAGECOACH

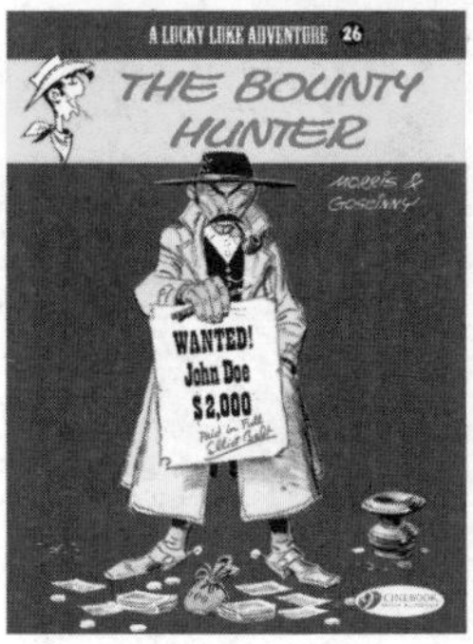
A LUCKY LUKE ADVENTURE 26
THE BOUNTY HUNTER
WANTED! John Doe $2,000

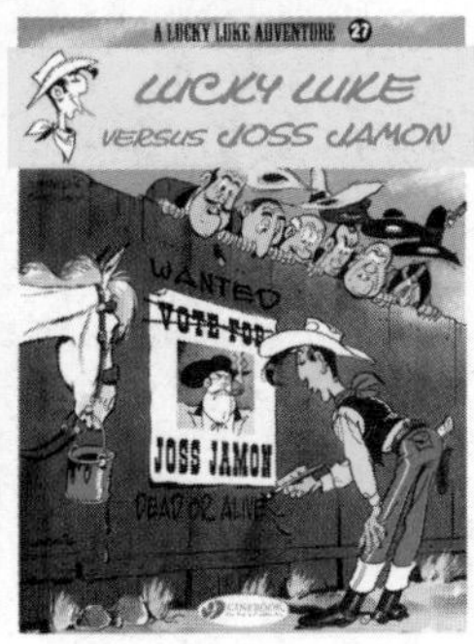
A LUCKY LUKE ADVENTURE 27
LUCKY LUKE VERSUS JOSS JAMON
JOSS JAMON

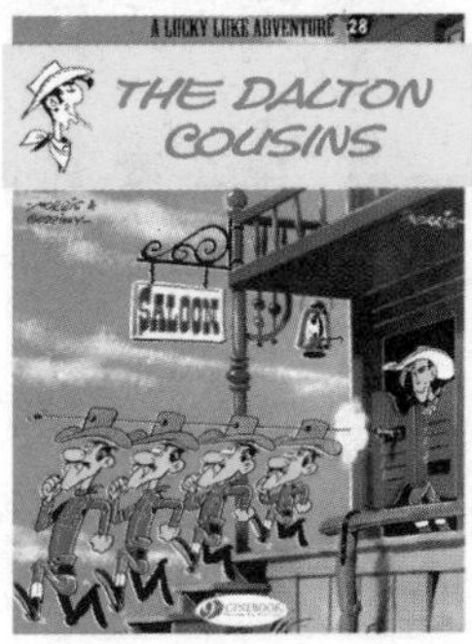
A LUCKY LUKE ADVENTURE 28
THE DALTON COUSINS
SALOON

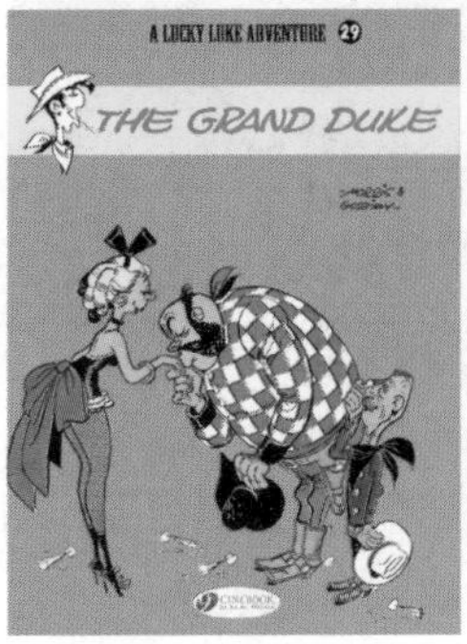
A LUCKY LUKE ADVENTURE 29
THE GRAND DUKE

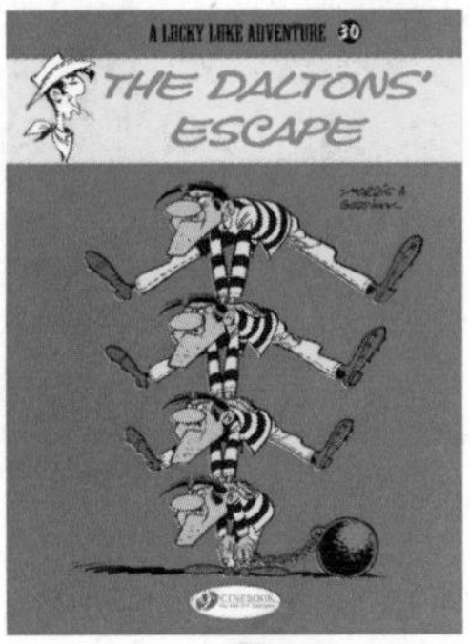
A LUCKY LUKE ADVENTURE 30
THE DALTONS' ESCAPE

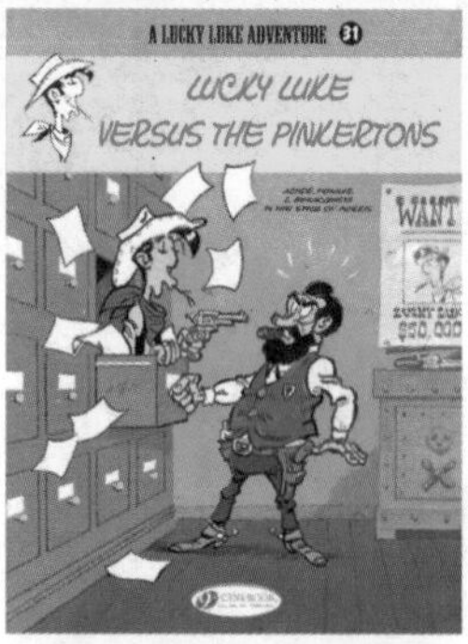
A LUCKY LUKE ADVENTURE 31
LUCKY LUKE VERSUS THE PINKERTONS

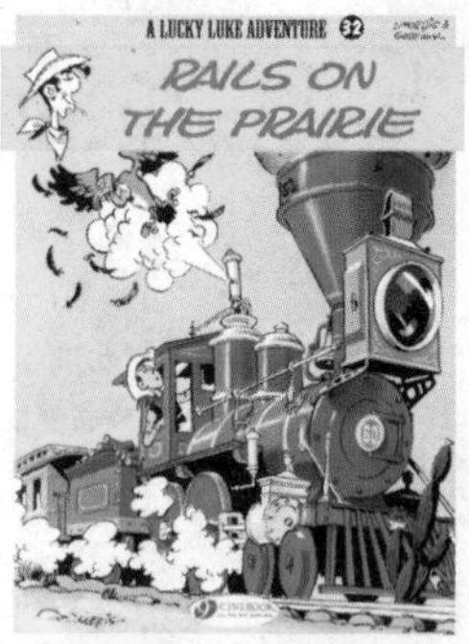
A LUCKY LUKE ADVENTURE 32
RAILS ON THE PRAIRIE

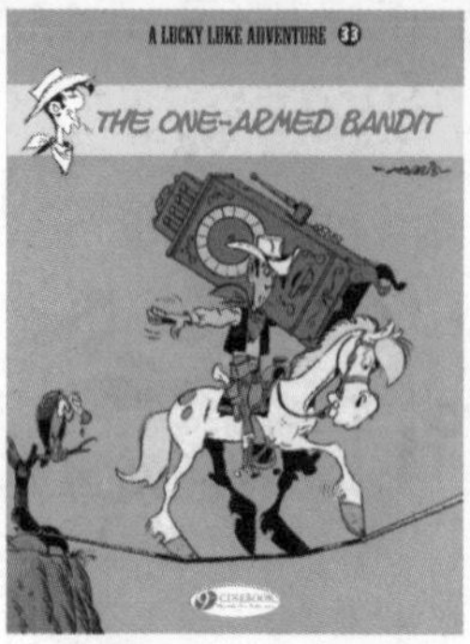
A LUCKY LUKE ADVENTURE 33
THE ONE-ARMED BANDIT

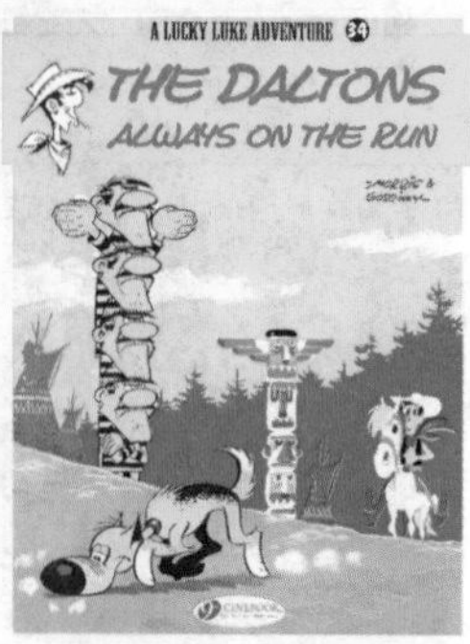
A LUCKY LUKE ADVENTURE 34
THE DALTONS ALWAYS ON THE RUN

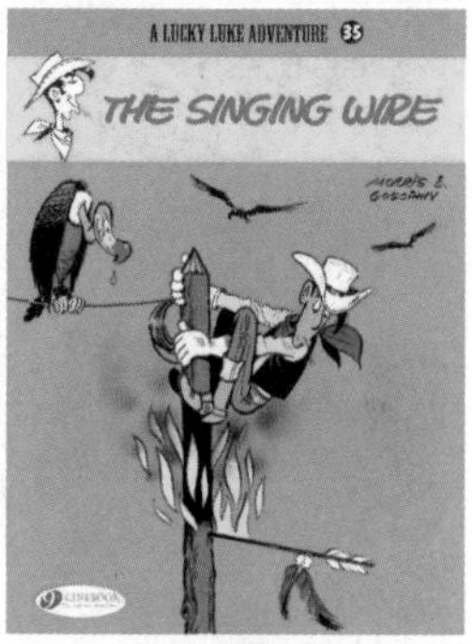
A LUCKY LUKE ADVENTURE 35
THE SINGING WIRE

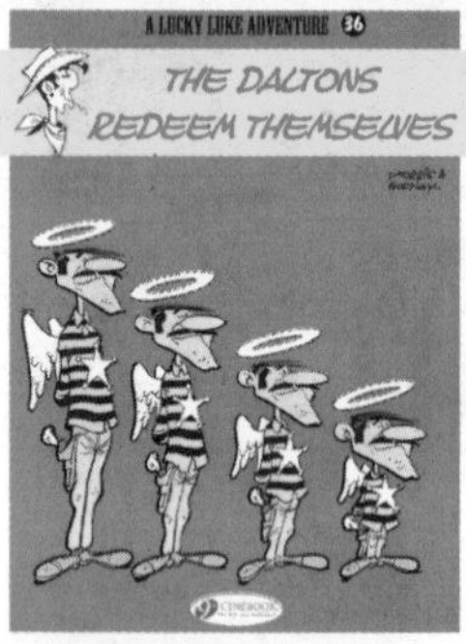
A LUCKY LUKE ADVENTURE 36
THE DALTONS REDEEM THEMSELVES

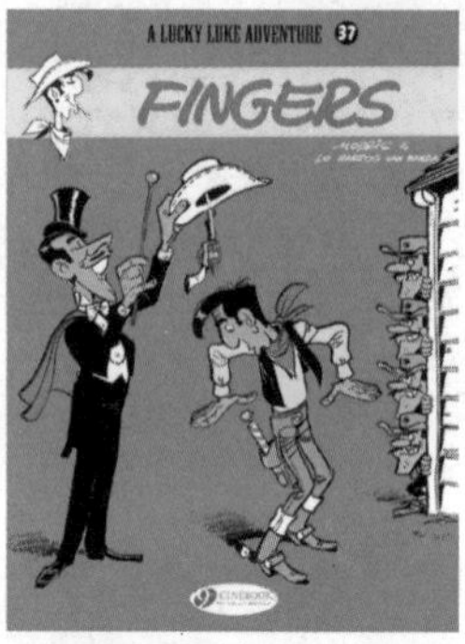
A LUCKY LUKE ADVENTURE 37
FINGERS

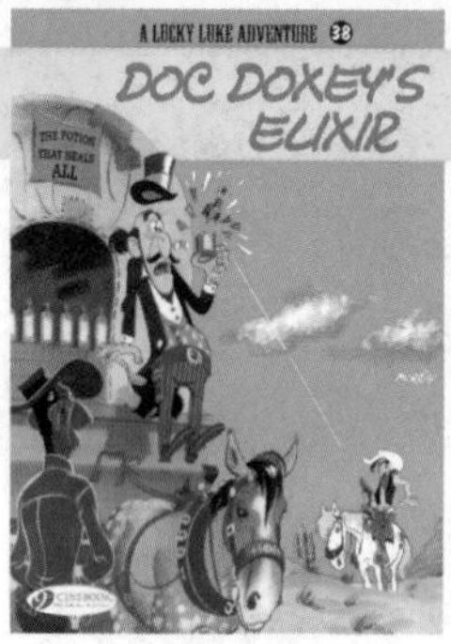
A LUCKY LUKE ADVENTURE 38
DOC DOXEY'S ELIXIR

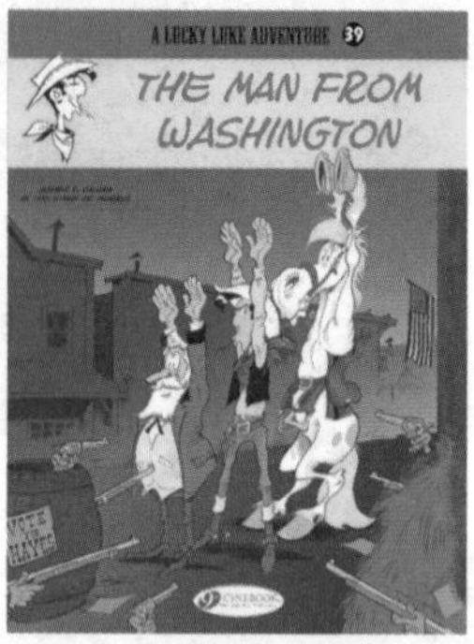
A LUCKY LUKE ADVENTURE 39
THE MAN FROM WASHINGTON

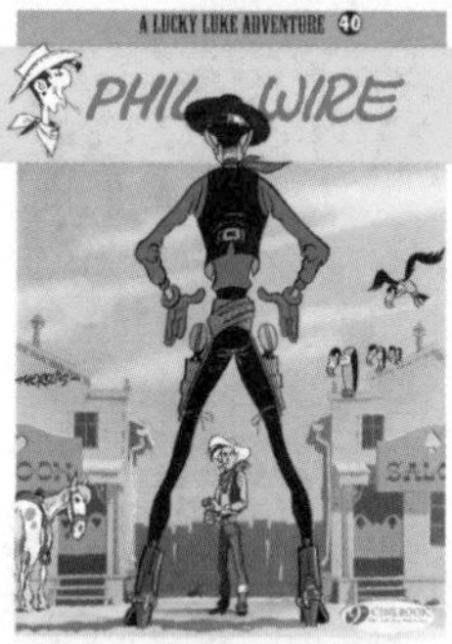
A LUCKY LUKE ADVENTURE 40
PHIL WIRE

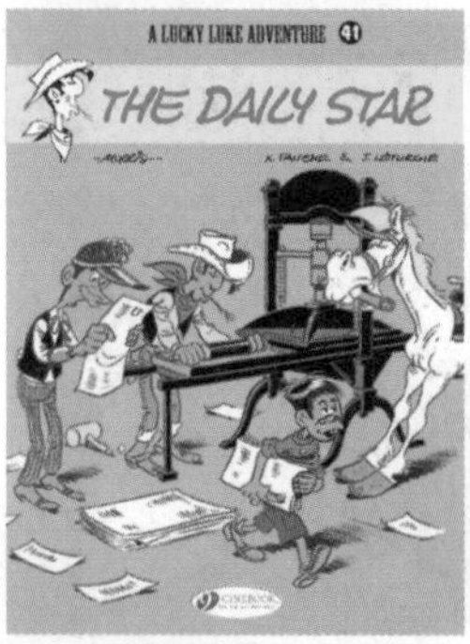
A LUCKY LUKE ADVENTURE 41
THE DAILY STAR

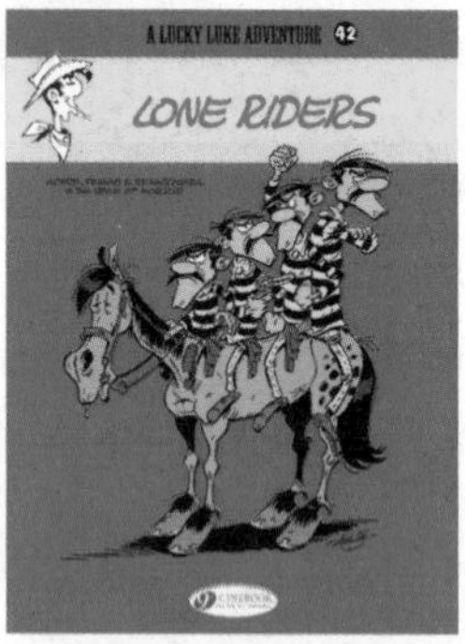
A LUCKY LUKE ADVENTURE 42
LONE RIDERS

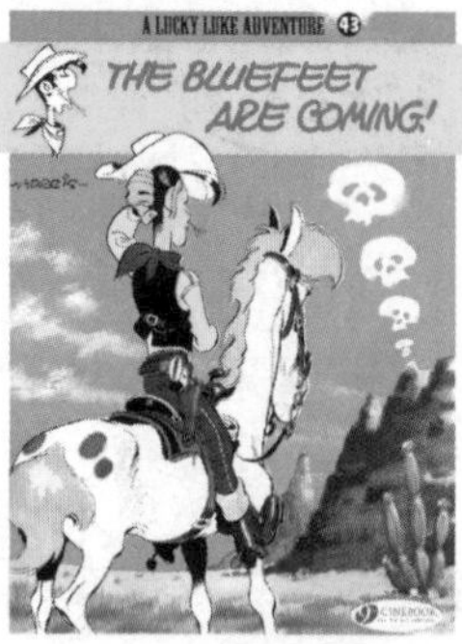
A LUCKY LUKE ADVENTURE 43
THE BLUEFEET ARE COMING!

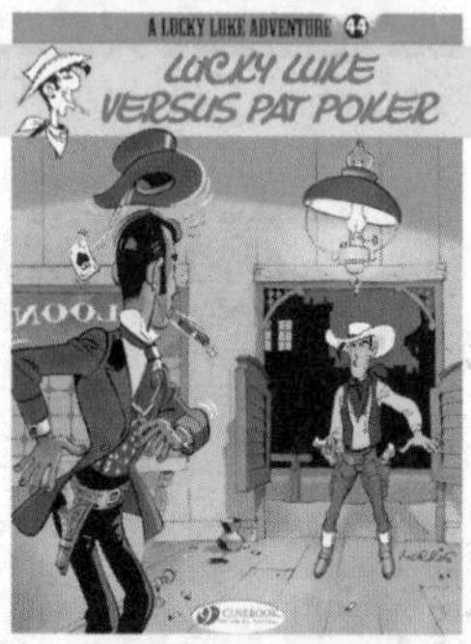
A LUCKY LUKE ADVENTURE 44
LUCKY LUKE VERSUS PAT POKER

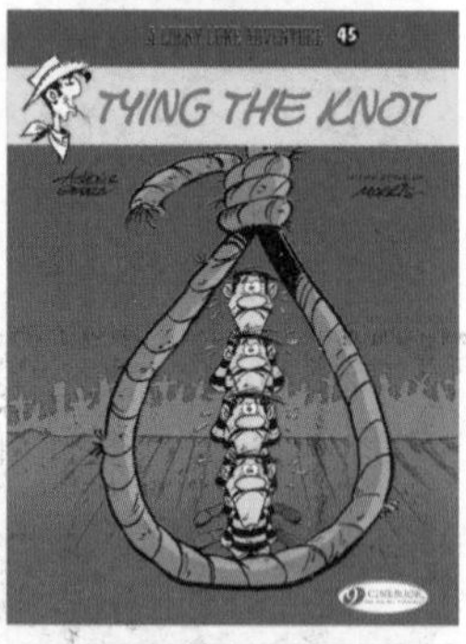
A LUCKY LUKE ADVENTURE 45
TYING THE KNOT

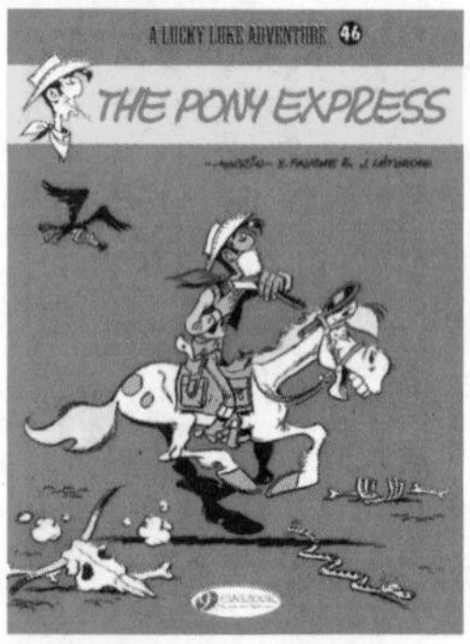
A LUCKY LUKE ADVENTURE 46
THE PONY EXPRESS

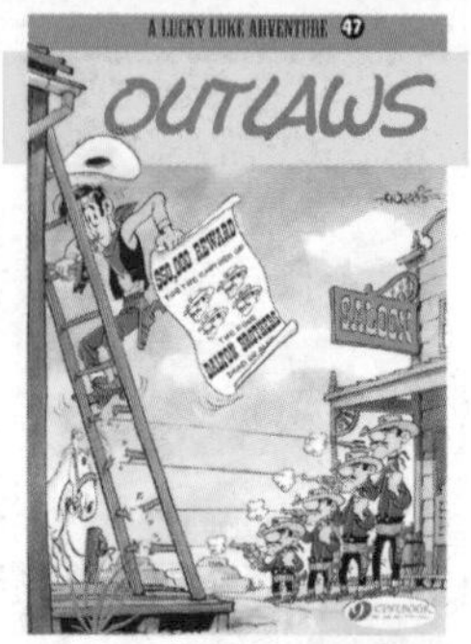
A LUCKY LUKE ADVENTURE 47
OUTLAWS

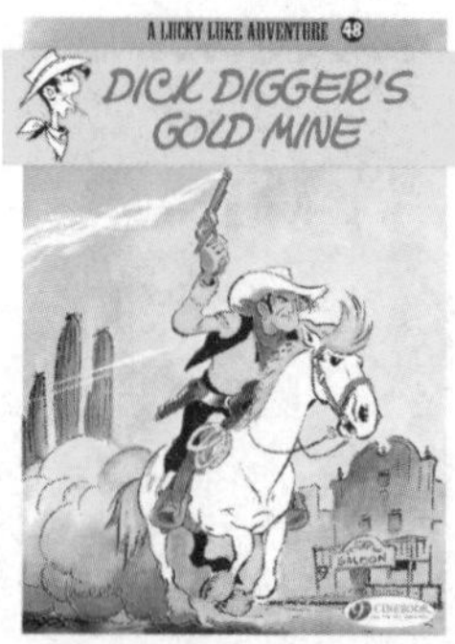
A LUCKY LUKE ADVENTURE 48
DICK DIGGER'S GOLD MINE

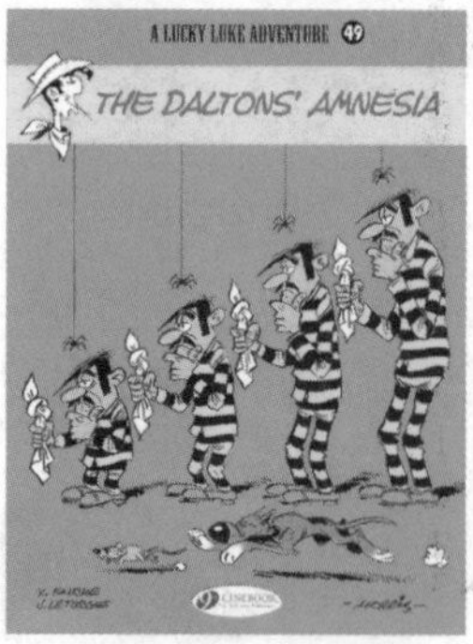
A LUCKY LUKE ADVENTURE 49
THE DALTONS' AMNESIA

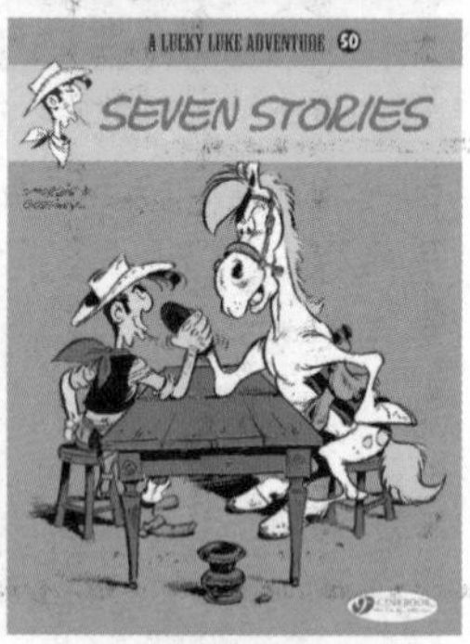
A LUCKY LUKE ADVENTURE 50
SEVEN STORIES

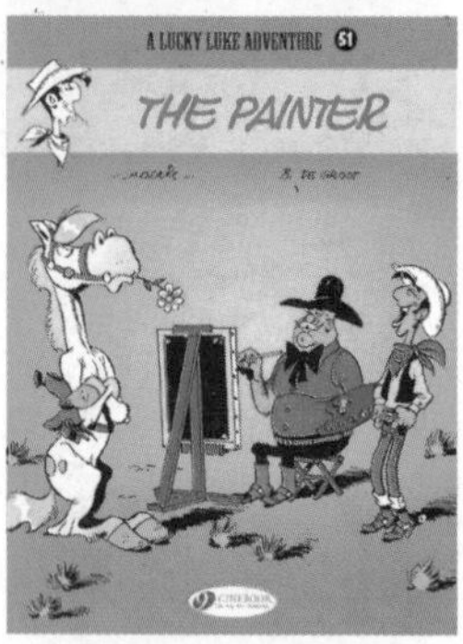
A LUCKY LUKE ADVENTURE 51
THE PAINTER

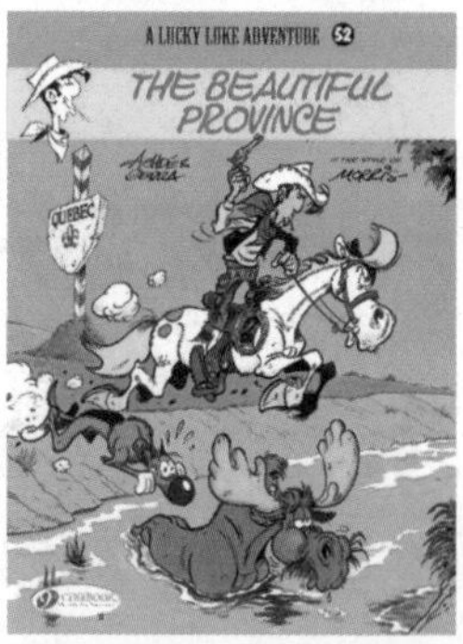
A LUCKY LUKE ADVENTURE 52
THE BEAUTIFUL PROVINCE

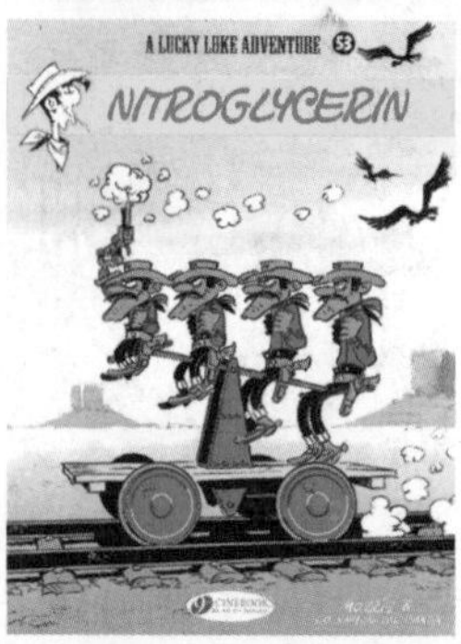
A LUCKY LUKE ADVENTURE 53
NITROGLYCERIN

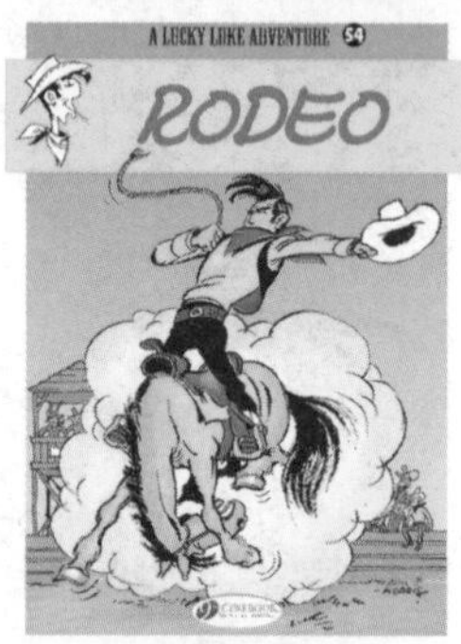
A LUCKY LUKE ADVENTURE 54
RODEO

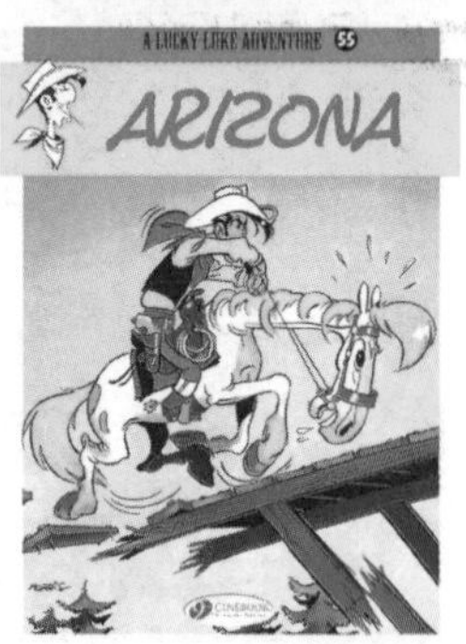
A LUCKY LUKE ADVENTURE 55
ARIZONA

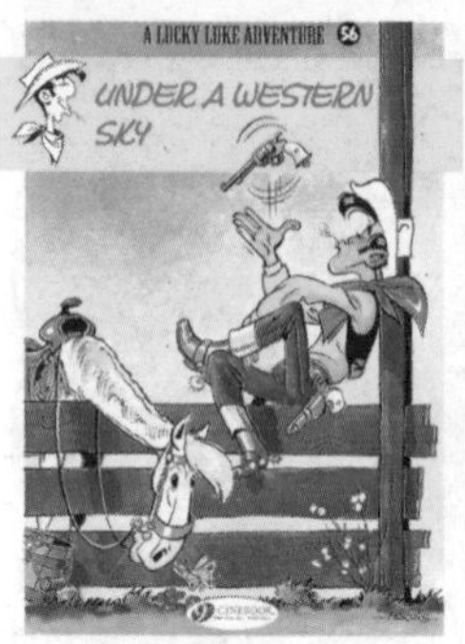
A LUCKY LUKE ADVENTURE 56
UNDER A WESTERN SKY

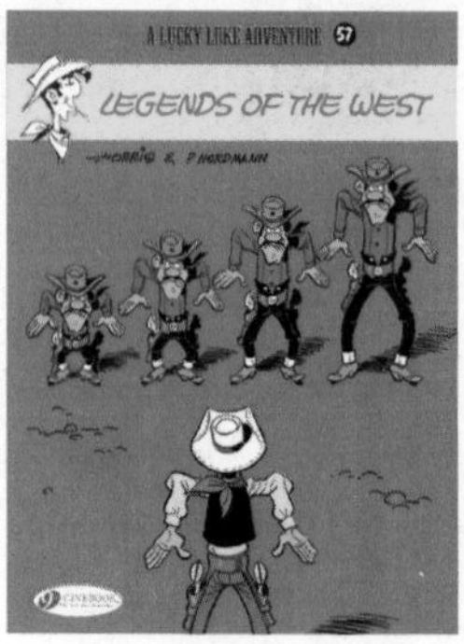
A LUCKY LUKE ADVENTURE 57
LEGENDS OF THE WEST

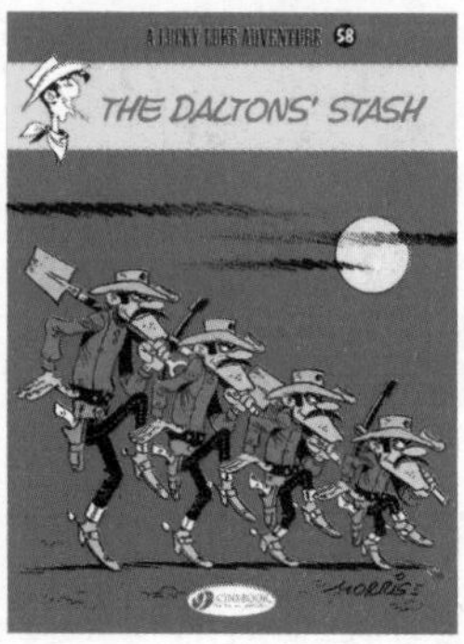
A LUCKY LUKE ADVENTURE 58
THE DALTONS' STASH

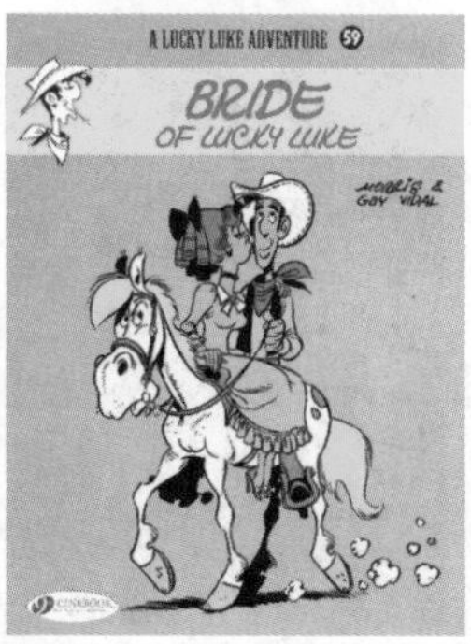
A LUCKY LUKE ADVENTURE 59
BRIDE OF LUCKY LUKE

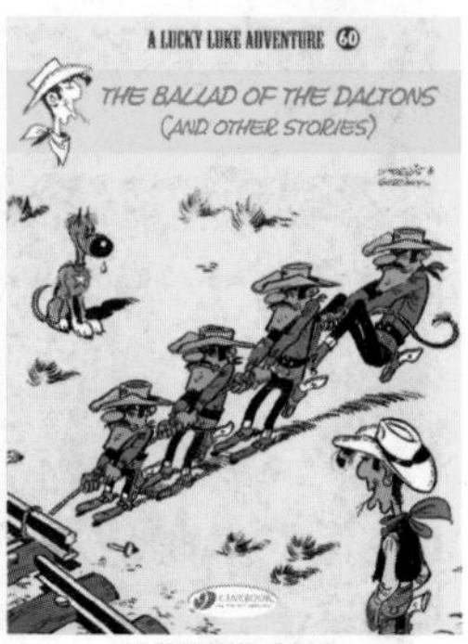
A LUCKY LUKE ADVENTURE 60
THE BALLAD OF THE DALTONS (AND OTHER STORIES)

JUNE 2016

AUGUST 2016